The
Conspiracy
of
Compassion

The Conspiracy of Compassion

Breathing Together for a Wounded World

Joseph Nassal, CPPS

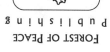

FOREST OF PEACE
Publishing

Suppliers for the Spiritual Pilgrim

The Conspiracy of Compassion

copyright © 1997, by Joseph Nassal

Library of Congress Cataloging-in-Publication Data
Nassal, Joe, 1955-
The conspiracy of compassion : breathing together for a wounded world / Joseph Nassal.
    p. cm.
    ISBN 0-939516-34-9 (pbk.)
    1. Caring--Religious aspects--Christianity.   I. Title
BV4647.S9N37 1997
248--dc21
                                          96-29841
                                          CIP

published by
Forest of Peace Publishing, Inc.
PO Box 269
Leavenworth, KS 66048-0269 USA
1-800-659-3227

printed by
Hall Commercial Printing
Topeka, KS 66608-0007

1st printing: January 1997
2nd printing: September 1998

cover art (reproduced with permission)
VATER UND SOHN • PÈRE ET FILS • FATHER AND SON
Ewald Mataré, Bronze.
ars liturgica KUNSTVERLAG MARIA LAACH (Germany) Nr. 5408

For my brother

Ed

April 10, 1949 – June 8, 1987

Indictments

I charge the following people with conspiracy to commit crimes of compassion. They are the ones who have breathed new life, new stories, and new hope in me. I will always be grateful to them: Edward Hays, Mark Miller, Alan Hartway, Tren Meyers, Jack McClure, Bill Huebsch, Chris Ostmeyer, Dave Kelly, Bill Nordenbrock, Dennis Kinderman, the members and companions of the Kansas City Province of the Congregation of the Most Precious Blood, Lucy and Rollie Reznicek, Adrian and Lorraine Ramos, and the late Patricia Bishop. I also acknowledge with gratitude Father Carroll Stuhlmueller, CP, who died in February, 1994. As a teacher and mentor of mine, Carroll's love for Scripture left an indelible imprint on my soul.

I am also deeply grateful to so many people in places where I have been privileged to minister — Centerville, IA, Sedalia, MO, St. Joseph, MO, Davenport, IA, Liberty, MO and Kansas City, MO — and the many people in places and parishes where I have given retreats and missions who have shared their stories of pain and promise with me over the years.

In the summer of 1995 I moved to Shantivanam, the House of Prayer for the Archdiocese of Kansas City, Kansas in Easton, Kansas. Here I have been privileged to follow my mentor and friend, the founder of Shantivanam, Father Ed Hays, as director. The committed community of lay women and men have taught me more than I ever thought I could hold about what it means to be inclusive and compassionate. I am deeply grateful to Jennifer Sullivan, Joanne Meyer, Tom Turkle, Tom and Jan Skorupa, Phyllis DeMey, Monica Hutton, Tom and Beth Jacobs, Don and Elizabeth Schmidling, Josie LeCluyse, Tom and Mary Pineau, and the many friends of the Forest of Peace who support the ministry of prayer. I am especially grateful to my editor, Tom Skorupa, who breathed new life into this manuscript, and my publisher, Tom Turkle, for his generous guidance and friendship.

Finally, and most importantly, to my mom and dad, Doris and Joe Nassal, my sisters, Sharon and Mary, and my brother, Bob: We have shared much laughter and love over the years, but when Ed died, you taught me how to love even in the losing.

Contents

Thus says God:
"Come from the four winds, O breath,
and breathe upon these slain,
that they may live."

– Ezekiel 37: 9

The morning wind spreads its fresh smell.
We must wake up and take it in,
this wind that lets us live.
Breathe before it's gone.

Dance, when you're broken open.
Dance, if you've torn the bandage off.
Dance in the middle of the struggle.
Dance in your blood.
Dance, when you're perfectly free.

– Rumi

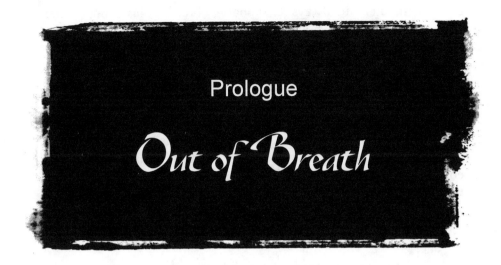

Prologue

Out of Breath

When I was a child and scraped my knee or scratched my arm or suffered some sort of abrasion to my skin, my mom would put this red stuff (that's what I called it since I couldn't pronounce its real name) on the wound and then blow on it. It heals better if you blow on it, Mom would say. It was true: Her gentle breath would take some of the sting away.

On June 8, 1987, a wound was inflicted on my family that took our breath away. On that morning, my brother Ed, who for more than a decade endured the insidious illness of paranoid schizophrenia, went to the basement of my parents' home, secured a gun in the vise on my father's workbench, wrapped his mouth around the barrel of the gun and pulled the trigger.

On that Monday morning, the only thing out of the routine that Ed followed each day since the onset of his illness was that he took a shower shortly after getting up at 6:00. Since Monday was the day he normally mowed the lawn, Mom wondered why he was taking a shower. But she didn't think much about it and said good-bye to him as she left for St. Ferdinand's Church where she worked as a secretary.

"Good-bye, Mom," Ed said. It was 8:10.

We never forget the last words a person speaks before he or she dies. My mother will always remember my brother's last words to her as she left for work. She did not catch the finality of those two words, "Good-bye, Mom." It is a common enough expression. She expected it meant, "See you later." But for Ed it meant, "It is finished."

Two hours later, he was dead.

Dad had retired a few months before and had begun a ritual of walking every morning right after Mom left for work. He left the house at 8:15. When he returned home at about 10:30, the house was warmer than it should have been. They had been having trouble with the air conditioner, so Dad went downstairs to check it out. There he found Ed, his oldest son, lying in a pool of blood.

Ed used to hunt, so we knew there were guns in the house. But a few years before, he had given all the shells to Mom to throw away. All but one.

Could we see this coming? Possibly. For eleven years we could see it coming. The doctors had told us that Ed was not suicidal though it was always a possibility with patients diagnosed with paranoid schizophrenia. I guess it's a familiar lament — we thought it would never happen to us. In fact, such a possibility was the farthest thing from our minds on Sunday afternoon, the day before. My Aunt Louise and Uncle Red were visiting that day, and Ed was euphoric as he cheered the St. Louis baseball Cardinals home to victory. He seemed excited about my moving back to St. Louis later that summer to begin graduate studies at St. Louis University and told Mom that he was looking forward to going to some Cardinal games with me. Before he went to bed that night, he told Mom that he might try again to get a part-time job. He had tried various jobs since his schizophrenia was diagnosed, but they only lasted a few days or a few weeks at best.

The last time I saw Ed was the Monday after Easter. We played golf, and I remember being so frustrated because the course was crowded and Ed kept apologizing for his poor play. On June 8, 1987, I was playing golf again at the annual Clergy Day golf tournament in Jefferson City. We had just finished the tenth hole. A priest who was not playing in our foursome approached the green in a golf cart just as we were putting out. He stood by one of the priests I was playing with, and as I lined up my putt I saw him whisper in my playing partner's ear. As I was walking off the green, the priest came up to me and said there had been an emergency and the bishop wanted to see me right away.

When I arrived in the clubhouse, the bishop was standing at the starter's counter. Michael McAuliffe is a kind and gentle man, a very pastoral and compassionate bishop. But now he had the terrible responsibility of telling me that my brother was dead. In a very soft voice, he told me my brother had been shot and offered to take me to his residence a few blocks away to call my family for more details.

Sharon, my oldest sister, answered the phone. I could tell immediately by the tone of her voice that in this case "being shot" and "being dead" were synonymous. But I had to hear her say it.

"He's gone, Joe, he's gone."

Bishop McAuliffe was waiting for me when I finished talking with Sharon. We talked briefly — I told him about Ed and the pain he had endured the past few years. The bishop was most understanding and compassionate. But I was in a hurry to leave and begin the journey home. Bishop Michael sent me on my way with the promise of his prayer for me and my family.

As I drove home, I turned up the volume on the car stereo as if the sound could drown out my thoughts. It almost worked except that one thought kept time in my mind: how I missed Ed already — and how often I missed him while he was alive.

Late that same night after all the family was in bed, I went downstairs to the basement. I noticed a half-empty pack of cigarettes on the table outside Ed's room. Ed smoked Winstons. It looked as if he had finished two cigarettes and started on a third but snuffed it out. I sat there staring at that ashtray, trying to catch my breath.

Mom's miracle cure with the red stuff would not work now. This wound was too deep. Ed's suicide cut far beneath the surface of the skin to that space we call the soul. Though I could not put words on the feeling then, Ed's death had knocked the wind out of me. I was doubled-over, gasping, and desperately grasping for a prayer or a second wind.

There were no remedies to the wound inflicted by Ed's death. Yet during the next few weeks, and often during the next few years, I discovered there is a sacred wind that blows within us and beckons us to believe. That wind is carried in the gentle breath of others who are willing to share our pain. It is found in the calm, cool breeze of a spring morning as one sits on the shore of a lake. It is heard in the whisper of a friend who reminds us we are not alone. It is felt deep in one's soul when one knows that the answer to our every prayer lies in the love we are willing to share with each other.

In the gentle murmur of this sacred wind, a conspiracy is born. It is a conspiracy of compassion.

Though for many the word conspiracy conveys the sense of an evil plot that threatens established institutions — like Watergate or Iran-Contra in recent times — this book seeks to reclaim the original meaning of *conspire*: to breathe together. The conspiracy of compassion captures our breathing together for goodness' sake. From a Christian perspective, followers of Jesus Christ are to be "co-conspirators" in the sacred story of salvation. We breathe together not for evil but for good; not for ruin but for redemption; not for the upper hand but for the lowest place.

The Hebrew and Christian Scriptures are full of stories about God's sacred wind — from the first moment of creation when the Spirit of God moved across the waters and created order out of chaos through that day when the early disciples of Jesus were gathered in the house and they heard a sound "like the rush of a mighty wind" that blew them away and out the door to speak new languages and live in love. We know these stories by heart: the ancient mariner, Noah, his family and two representatives of all living creatures that carried within them "the breath of life"; the long arm of the passionate prophet Moses, who "stretched out his hand over the sea" while God sent "a strong east wind" to create a wall of water that allowed the chosen ones to find their freedom; the handsome young shepherd, David, chosen by God and consecrated when "the Spirit of the Lord came mightily" upon him; the vision and voice of the fiery prophets like Ezekiel who saw the valley of dead, dry bones but could sense the air moving about him and could hear God saying to those bones, "Behold, I will cause breath to enter you, and you shall live"; and the incarnation of God's compassion in the person of Jesus who breathed his last on a cross outside the gates of the holy city only to return three days later to that upper room, his wounds visible, to breathe new life into his fearful followers.

We inherit the wind in these sacred stories when we leave our wounds open to the gentle breath of God's Spirit. When we open the battered shutters of our souls and inhale the fresh air of this Spirit, we are renewed. When we then breathe together as compassionate companions for peace, our world is renewed.

This book will not try to trap the sacred wind that breathes within each of us and blows all around us so much as tap the hallowed history of the wind as Holy Spirit who goes where the wind wills but always breathes first and last on the wounds of our lives.

Just as my mom blew on my wounded knee when I was a boy, so our God breathes upon our scarred hearts. And when we are exposed to this sacred breeze, we come to know that even though we may not be able to catch the wind, we can catch our breath again.

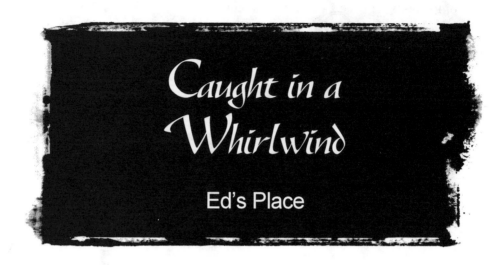

Caught in a Whirlwind

Ed's Place

The Book of Genesis begins by describing the sacred wind we will be reflecting on in these pages. The story says that God started from scratch. There was nothing but a deep darkness. But then the Spirit Wind of God swept across this abyss, and out of nothingness came the light.

Chaos. That word captures well what my brother Ed's life had become. Mental illness had thrown him into a deep and dark abyss. For the last eleven years of his life, he never saw the light. In sharp contrast to his inner environment those last years is the scene surrounding his cabin at the Lake of the Ozarks, marked by a sign carved in wood that says simply, "Ed's Place." This little corner of creation was Ed's refuge, his sanctuary, his safe harbor from the storms of life. But as beautiful and peaceful as it is there, Ed could never escape the chaotic chasm that had swallowed him. He could never really be free from the mental anguish that raged inside.

Until Monday, June 8, 1987.

We can trace the first time when Ed's mind began to go awry. It was Easter Sunday night in 1976, my twenty-first birthday. The family had gathered at Aunt Louise and Uncle Red's as tradition dictated. I wasn't there since I was in the seminary at the time and we didn't get an

Easter break in those days.

After dinner, as was and still is the custom, the family started playing pinochle. Everyone was having a good time and there were some good-natured comments about Ed still being single. No one ever took these seriously because Ed had always been a free spirit. He was twenty-seven, bright, talented, had a good job, and he would get married when he was ready.

Ed got up from the pinochle table that Easter Sunday evening and went outside. When he didn't return for the next hand, Sharon went looking for him. Ed and Sharon had always been close, since they were born less than a year apart. They grew up together and there was a special bond between them. Sharon found Ed sitting in his car. He was crying and mumbling something about how no one loved him, how all the family talked behind his back. He sounded confused and afraid.

This was the beginning — the first real evidence that any of us can recall of Ed's incarceration in the prison of mental illness.

In the days, weeks and months that followed, all of us sorted through our memories looking for clues. What could we have said or done to spark this strange and inexplicable behavior? Was it the jokes about Ed not being married? We tried with all our energy to place blame, for we were confronted with an illness beyond the realm of reason. Since I was away at school during the earliest stages of Ed's condition, I wasn't directly involved in what was happening. But when I got home in May of that year, I remember how Ed would walk into the family room and accuse us of talking about him. Nothing we could say to Ed would convince him otherwise. He had heard voices and they were real. But they weren't coming from the family room; they were coming from inside his head.

My first real confrontation with the demons raging inside Ed's mind occurred in June of that year. Thinking that perhaps Ed was under too much stress at work (he was in the National Guard and employed full-time as a mechanic at St. Louis International Airport), Mom and Dad invited him to go to Texas with us on what turned out to be our last vacation as a family. An old Navy buddy of Dad's had invited us to Galveston where he had a summer home on the Gulf of Mexico.

The trip down went well. Ed did most of the driving and nothing seemed out of the ordinary. "Back to the old Ed," became our rallying cry of hope in those times when Ed appeared back to "normal." By this time, though, all of us were watching our words and were tentative in our responses to Ed, unsure of what to say or how to respond for fear of "upsetting" him.

As soon as we arrived, Dad's friend invited us to take a spin in his boat on the gulf. Ed took the helm — he always enjoyed boats and the water and loved to water-ski. He seemed happy guiding the boat through the crashing waves with the hot sun beating down on his shoulders and the smell and taste of the salty water splashing his face. But that night, after we cleaned up, Ed announced that he had to go back to St. Louis. With anxiety in his voice and fear in his eyes, he told us he could not stay.

Mom, Dad, and I tried to reason with him, asking him to at least spend the night. "You'll feel better in the morning," we told him. But nothing we said would change Ed's mind. When Ed went to pack his things, we apologized to our host, saying that "Ed just hasn't been himself lately."

Our vacation had begun with the illness rearing its ugly head once again. It would be an appearance that would become all too common but never routine in the decade that followed.

Though we were frustrated and angry that Ed had suddenly spoiled the beginning of our vacation, those emotions would be replaced by fear as the months dragged on and Ed's illness became more familiar yet unfathomable. Our anxiety increased as we saw the illness shatter so many of our hopes and dreams for him and send the normal flow of our family life spinning into chaos.

Living in the Shadows

As we struggled with our own responses to Ed's sudden shift in personality, we also wondered what other people — especially our relatives — must have thought about Ed's odd behavior. Though he was still working, the illness was gradually taking over every phase of his life, his relationships, his world.

Ed was one of the pallbearers at my grandmother's funeral in October of that first year. He looked terrible that day. His eyes were glassy and he stared into space. The illness had made him barely functional. He left immediately after the burial rather than going to my cousin's house for a gathering of the family. My relatives voiced their concern about Ed. We didn't know what to tell them. It was obvious that something was terribly wrong with Ed. Some suspected he might be on drugs. But we dismissed these charges quickly and defiantly. Shortly after Gram's funeral, Ed was hospitalized for the first time.

I remember visiting him at the psychiatric center with Mom. I had just seen the film "One Flew Over the Cuckoo's Nest," so all the images from that movie of what life was like inside a mental hospital were etched in my memory as we went up the front steps. I glanced quickly at some of the other patients who wandered the corridors or sat on the steps as we walked toward Ed's room, hoping they wouldn't catch me staring. I was in awe at how mysterious the mind is that allowed these people to spend their days and nights in such quiet desperation.

Ed received shock treatments while he was in the hospital. The electric charges to the brain destroyed some of his memory. After such treatments, Ed would sit for hours paging through the photo albums at home trying to remember the events that the pictures captured. Or he would go to the basement with Dad's old Bell and Howell movie projector and watch the home movies, worn with age, that Dad had made for so many years when we were growing up. But the images on the screen did not help to replace the pieces of memory drowned by the shock waves.

I never knew what to say to Ed when I visited him in the hospital. I was saved from frequent visits because I was always away at school, or, after ordination, assigned to a parish far enough away from St. Louis that weekend trips or overnight visits seemed impractical. Or so I thought. The time he spent at these institutions did not last long — sometimes a few days; other times a few weeks. But for Ed, the minutes must have painfully plodded by. For the rest of us, these hospital stays were ominous reminders that Ed's illness was incurable.

The medication would work for awhile and keep Ed balanced temperamentally, but he was never able to go back to work once the National Guard retired him. He was never able to concentrate at any one thing for very long. His mouth was always dry, and he would suck on hard candy as he walked around the house in his old blue bathrobe. Sometimes he walked the house as if in a daze, shuffling his feet, a Winston smoldering in his hand, never saying a word.

The darkest moment during those years was the day in the spring of 1983 when Ed threatened his doctor with physical violence. After Ed left the office and returned home, the police came to the door to take him into custody and have him committed to yet another mental institution. The most difficult day, until June 8, 1987 at least, in my mom's life was that day when she stood in the courtroom and signed the papers to have her son committed.

Nailed to a Cross

As Ed's condition persisted and Mom's letters from home each week documented the deterioration of his mind and body, Ed became the focus of my prayer in my first year after ordination. Often at night when I would go over to lock up the church, I would sit on the sanctuary floor in the dark and the silence. I would lean against the pulpit and fix my eyes on the sanctuary lamp. The lamp shed a narrow glow around the crucifix. The body of Jesus was faintly illuminated in the dim light. Ed was being crucified by this illness. As Jesus was silent before his tormenters as he hung from the cross, so was Ed. And my prayer was always the same: "Take Ed down from the cross! He's hung on this cross long enough! Let him experience Easter."

But Ed never made it beyond Good Friday.

One night I will never forget was a year or so after I was ordained when I was living in Centerville, Iowa. I had received a letter from my mom that day reflecting her frustration at not knowing what to do or how to reach Ed. Mom had to tell him to take a shower and change his clothes. He sat around all day and stared "like a zombie," Mom wrote. She felt trapped by his silence. His frozen gaze pierced her heart. As I sat with my back to the pulpit and looked up at the crucifix hanging on the wall behind the altar, I remember thinking, "Is this what Jesus meant when he said one had to turn one's back on one's family, take up one's cross, and follow me?" I felt guilty that ever since the onset of Ed's illness I was always living away from home — first in the seminary and then, after ordination, in parish work far removed from my family in St. Louis. Certainly this wasn't what Jesus had in mind. I mean, is this what we are supposed to do: abandon family, those we love the most? It didn't make any sense. Ed's illness didn't make any sense. Priesthood for me didn't make any sense. Here I was ministering in a small Iowa parish, and those weekly letters from home reminded me of a suffering I could only dare to imagine and barely appreciate.

And so that night, I sat with my back to the pulpit and stared at the crucifix. Sunday after Sunday I preached from that pulpit to the good people of that parish, many of whom had allowed me into their suffering, their pain, and yes, into their experience of the promise and joy as well. As I prayed, I realized that while these people listened to my words and watched me, they also had a clear vision of the large crucifix behind the altar. They beheld the crucifix that captured their faith, that brought them to church. They beheld the outstretched arms of Jesus on the cross that gathered them around the table. The very crucifix I had my back to every time I preached now transfixed me. Imprinted on my soul, it was an image that would live foremost in my consciousness for years to come.

Later that week, one of the few friends with whom I had shared about Ed's illness sent me a story about a young man named Eric. He was a paranoid schizophrenic, and the article detailed the devastating effects his illness had on his family. As I read Eric's story, the remarkable similarities with Ed's story moved me deeply. Though the onset of Ed's problems started much later than Eric's (and were not nearly as severe as yet), the response of the family to Eric was the same as ours had been: telling Ed to shape up, get a job, get some self-confidence and get on with his life — as if Ed (or Eric) were able to do any of those things. The shock treatments did not seem to help.

The article about Eric was a watershed of sorts for me in understanding and being able to talk about Ed's illness to others. Until this time, Ed's illness had been for the most part a "family secret." The closest relatives knew there was something terribly wrong with Ed but never pried to know more. It had been almost seven years since Ed first showed signs of schizophrenia. He was no longer working. He was living at home. He avoided all family gatherings. He even missed my ordination, leaving early on the morning I was to be ordained and going to the lake. He left me a note to congratulate me, telling me how sorry he was but he just couldn't handle all the people being around. I was disappointed, of course, and probably a little angry. But I was too nervous that morning to give it too much thought. It was only later when the pictures from the ordination came back (and especially the pictures of the family together) that Ed's absence that day left a wound.

By this time Ed had lost touch with most of his friends. Some people knew something was wrong, but as it often seems with mental disease, people kept their distance. What can one say? What can one do? It's not that they were indifferent to Ed's suffering; it was just that they felt as impotent as we did.

I entrusted Ed's story to a few close friends, asking for their prayers but realizing they were as powerless as anyone else to help. I guess I wanted them to know of Ed and my family's struggles and just hold us in prayer.

Let Him Go Free

Ed was committed to a mental institution by the courts in early March of 1983. At last we were becoming resigned to the reality that he would be this way for the rest of his life. This was an awesome realization because we had always held out the hope that Ed would return to his former way of life. After all, for twenty-seven years we had come to know and love Ed. But this was no longer the Ed we knew and even though we loved him as a brother and a son, it was difficult to accept that Ed would be "this way" for the rest of his life.

Being with Ed on family holidays — Thanksgiving, Christmas, Easter — was the most difficult family circumstance because he had become a shell of his former self. His silent presence aroused a wave of fear and frustration. We were continually confronted with our inability to confront or control or do anything about the terrible disease that raged inside his mind. Still, how much I would give to have his silent presence with us today. Not that we would be any better in dealing with his illness. It's just that his absence now is more deafening than his silence was during all those years when he was unable to experience the joy we were together to celebrate.

I am convinced that it was Mom's faith that helped all of us get through those most painful months; indeed, those eleven years. I became more aware than ever of seeing God's presence even in the suffering. Perhaps I had never really suffered before and that's why it took so long to realize that God was present even in those darkest moments. I came to understand and believe in a God who weeps with us — and weep we did.

When Jesus came to the tomb of his dead friend Lazarus, he wept. Though he knew Lazarus would come shuffling out of that tomb, seeing the tears of Mary, Martha and the others, he was moved to compassion. Just for a moment he imagined what life would be like without his friend. And then, when he told them to remove the stone and Lazarus came out of the tomb, Jesus told them to untie him and let him go free. How I prayed that what Jesus did for his friend Lazarus he would do for Ed. Let him go free. But my prayer went unanswered. At least I never received the answer for which I was looking.

For me, Ed's illness symbolized all the confusion and chaos of the world. The torn remnants of humanity were seen in the anguish of one man struggling to be free. There were no answers, no cures, for what was raging inside Ed's mind. There were no solutions, no easy avenues of escape from his awful reality until June 8, 1987 when Ed finally silenced the voices.

The Conspiracy Begins

On one level this book is my attempt to make some sense out of suffering. If I could go back and change any day in my life, it would be June 8, 1987, the day my brother Ed committed suicide. I am struck by that phrase, "committed suicide." For my brother, it was a commitment. He did not attempt it; he was committed to silencing the voices he had heard the last eleven years of his life. Since Ed's death, I have struggled with the question, "Why?" In reflecting on Ed's life and death, I have come to realize there is no single answer to that question, nor is there a satisfactory solution to the mystery of suffering. This is the point of the Paschal Mystery: We live through the suffering to find hope and life again.

In living into that Mystery, we are all inevitably wounded, initiated as it were into Christ's passion and into his way of compassion. As we live into that Mystery, we realize that recognizing our wounds is a prerequisite for recognizing and embracing the wounds of another. The fruit of personal suffering is a more compassionate heart. Compassionate people are those who know what they have suffered. They use their experiences of suffering to reach out to others. This is the basis and motivation for compassion: one's own experiences of pain and suffering. When this important first step is taken, when each of us tears away the bandages and takes the risk to allow our wounds to breathe, we begin to conspire together for the healing of our world.

In the chaos caused by suffering, God's Spirit sweeps across the void in the same way as in the creation story in the book of Genesis. When excruciating pain or indescribable sorrow has knocked the wind out of us, leaving us bent over and out of breath, helping us catch our breath is the same Spirit as was present that day in the upper room of the Heartbreak Hotel where the followers and closest friends of the recently executed rabbi were huddled in fear.

Here is where the conspiracy really took shape. These disciples had been seen with the one who was crucified. They were with him when all those unforgettable miracles took place. Because they had been seen with him, they were sure their faces were plastered on placards all over town. So they decided to hide out for a few days until the air of suspicion blew over. Then they could quietly sneak out of town and get on with their lives.

But instead of growing suspicion, a howling wind blew open the door that had been locked and barred. One of the disciples screamed, "It's all over! We've been caught!" But as the wind settled, they turned their heads and opened their eyes. "We must be seeing things," they thought. "All this stress must be causing hallucinations!" Then one shrieked (as he had cried out a few months before when he saw someone walking toward their boat on the stormy lake), "It's a ghost!"

No, not a ghost, but Jesus. "Peace be with you," he said. He showed them his hands and side. The wounds were still fresh. "Peace be with you," he said again. Then he did a simple but remarkable thing: He breathed on them.

This was nothing less than the rebirth of creation. That tiny breath of the Crucified One sparked a primal memory. Do you remember the story of how God created the first humans? God breathed God's very Spirit into the man and into the woman and fashioned living beings. The Genesis story tells us that we carry within us the very breath of God.

But we have inhaled so much foul air over the years — the pollution of poverty and injustice, the vile fumes of violence and oppression, the smog of smugness and self-sufficiency, and the smoke of burning ruins and smoldering dreams — that our breathing is labored at best. We have experienced so much pressure on our lungs from the meanness of life that our breathing is constricted. We have put on so many layers of bandages to cover our wounds, to defend ourselves from being hurt again, that our wounds never have a chance to heal.

When Jesus entered that upper room, he taught the disciples a *new* breathing exercise. In the foul air that hung heavy over their heads, he freed them from the straightjackets of fear that locked their lungs. He filled their lungs with the fresh, light air of the Holy Spirit. Dreams danced in their minds again. Courage pulsed through their bodies, replacing the arthritis of inactivity with the intensity of a young sprinter ready to erupt from the starting blocks. Spring returned to their step even as they walked among the ruins of winter's discontent.

Death had been conquered forever. Life had returned in its original form. A new genesis had begun. A new covenant was born in the whisper of a gentle breeze. A new creation was carried in the breath of a nail-scarred carpenter from Nazareth. For this carpenter had stayed on the cross long enough to die, had stayed in the tomb long enough to remember, had stayed in the upper room long enough to breathe new life into decaying hearts and fearful minds.

Before Jesus entered that upper room, the disciples were as dry as a Kansas field in late July. They were out of breath. The crucifixion of their friend had kicked them in the stomach and knocked the wind out of them. They were still trying to catch their breath when the gale-like force of Jesus' Spirit knocked down the door of the room where they were hiding.

But now, the conspiracy was on! The essence of the conspiracy contained in that tiny breath whispered in that upper room two thousand years ago is alive today. It's alive in the breath of those who do not yield to the temptation to inhale the cold air of compromise but instead choose to exhale the warm breezes of compassion. All we need to learn to be co-conspirators is the simple breathing exercise the disciples learned in the Heartbreak Hotel: When God exhales, we inhale.

Breathing into One's Heart

The Chinese character for love combines two symbols, one for *breathing* and the other for *heart*. The definition for love is "breathing into one's heart." Contained within that tiny breath of Jesus in the upper room was the fullness of spirit and the grace of love and compassion. The breath that flowed from his mouth in the upper room seeped into the minds and hearts and bodies of those whose faith had deflated. This breath gave them a new lease on life. It was the breath that revived them.

In the upper room Jesus started the disciples breathing again. The fresh air of Jesus' Spirit allowed the blood to pulse through their bodies and rekindled the holy fires of love and struggle, passion and promise in their hearts.

During those days following Ed's death, my family received the same kind of heart-to-heart resuscitation, the same quality of spiritual CPR. One couple in particular administered this sacrament of sacred breathing. But they could only perform this corporal work of compassion because they knew their own pain.

It was Christmas Eve morning in 1983 when I first tasted their pain. A very close friend from the parish invited me to go with her to the cemetery to place flowers on the grave of her son. He had been killed two years before in an automobile accident when the van in which he was riding was hit by a drunk driver. I had always admired the great faith that she and her husband showed in not allowing the bitterness of their tragedy to consume them. Instead, they drew upon their suffering to help others who experienced the death of a loved one. Their ministry of grief-sharing in that small Iowa community generated hope in those they touched with their compassion and their care.

That Christmas Eve morning in 1983 was bitterly cold. The temperature with the wind chill was about thirty below zero. As we stood at her son's grave, wrapped in each other's arms to keep warm, she whispered, "You know, Joe, people keep asking me if all the children will be home for Christmas. And I want to scream: No! All the children will never ever be home for Christmas again!"

The woman shared with me her incurable wound. This woman of great faith invited me into her garden of pain. She was echoing the prayer of Jesus in the Garden of Gethsemane when he asked God to take the cup of pain away. Like Jesus, she was willing to drink from the cup of suffering, taste its bitter vintage, and then share its fruit with others.

Four years later, long after I had moved on to another parish, this woman and her husband drove three hundred miles to be with my family and me when my brother died. She was one of the first people I called with the news of my brother's suicide. I called her because she knew the pain my family (and especially my mom) was going through. She knew. I had asked only for her prayers for my mom and dad and family, knowing that her prayers would help sustain us in our sorrow.

But her prayer became flesh when she and her husband arrived at my parents' home the morning after my brother's death. They didn't stay long. They didn't have to. But they were there, with my family and me. When she put her arm around my mother, she knew. She knew. There stood two mothers who had lost their sons now lost in an embrace of sorrow. They knew the pain.

This couple learned the meaning of love in their own experiences of excruciating sorrow — the death of their son. With that incurable wound etched upon their souls, they breathed into our broken hearts. These two people ushered us into the conspiracy of compassion.

Tracing the Wound

Before we can begin to understand the meaning of compassion, we must be willing to trace our own wounds. I am not suggesting we wallow in our wounds, since such an obsession with grief can paralyze us. But rather than firmly affixing a sterile bandage over our wounds, we need to allow them to breathe. Real healing requires that our wounds be exposed to fresh air.

Society teaches us that when we have been hurt we need to "get over it and get on with our lives." What this book suggests is slightly different: We get *through* the pain of our lives, not over it or around it. Only in this way can we "get on with our lives." Only in this process can we be ministers of healing and hope for others — just as that woman and her husband were for my family and me.

The first question to ask always is: Where are our wounds? Only then can we even begin to address the second question: What do we do with our wounds?

Each of us is wounded in some way. We may be wounded by love in the betrayal of a close friend or wounded by greed in reaching for fame or personal glory. Perhaps the wound has been inflicted by the death of a loved one or the desecration of a dream. The wound might have been caused by the callousness of others or by our own lack of compassion. The wound may have resulted from changes in the church or society that happened too fast or are happening too slowly. Loss of our reputation or good name may have uncovered our shame and left us licking our wounds. Missed opportunities and misunderstandings can cause wounds that seem superficial at first but cut deeper than we realize.

Whatever the cause, our tendency is to reach for a bandage and cover the wound. But if the story of Jesus' appearance to the disciples after the resurrection teaches us anything, it says we must allow our wounds to breathe. The scars of the crucifixion were visible on the body of Jesus when he appeared to the disciples in the upper room. He showed them his scars so that they might believe. His wounds were his calling card, his identifying insignia, his birthmark.

The story says that only when our wounds are left open can healing take place. By tracing our wounds, we find the courage to accept who we are. We find our identity in our wounds. They mark our new birth.

To effectively trace our wounds we need to breathe into them, opening to their size and shape, their intensity and their source. It is never easy to embrace or even trace all of our wounds. But by breathing into the mysterious heart of our wounds, we expose them not only to the light of day, and to our own full awareness, but to the healing breath of the risen Christ in the upper room.

The only real answer to the prayer of a broken heart is the realization that God's heart has been broken. God knows our pain. God knows our suffering. God knows how difficult it is at times to catch our breath after we have been kicked in the stomach by tragedy or loss. God knows and responds. We find our home in the broken heart of God. And as we breathe deeply and prayerfully into the heart of our hurts, we breathe in not only the presence of a compassionate God, but the fresh air of the Spirit. It is the Spirit of the One who has gone through suffering, whose breath upon the disciples offers us the promise of suffering transformed into new life, into joy.

In my own search for meaning in experiences of suffering, I have come to believe that the only real healing for our deepest hurt is found in inhaling that divine breath which is often felt in the compassion we experience from others. When we leave our wounds exposed, another's gentle breath takes some of the sting out of our pain.

And it is when we know our own pain, our own suffering, our own experiences of sorrow that we find the courage and the sensitivity to breathe upon another's wound. In our wounds we discover our capacity for compassion. We allow our personal experiences of suffering to motivate us to be with others in their pain, in their suffering, in their sorrow. We learn to breathe deeply in the midst of our collective wounds. It is in our most devastating loss, our most excruciating pain, our deepest wound, that we discover what the poet Robert Bly has called our greatest gift to the community. Certainly, from a Christian perspective, this is borne out in the wounds visible on the body of Jesus after his resurrection. The Christian story of salvation says that in the wounds of the crucified and risen Christ we find healing. In the wounds of a crucified God, we are redeemed.

To sum up, then, the call to be compassionate extends an awesome challenge to us. It demands that we hold ourselves open and have the courage to look honestly at our own wounds, our own pain, our own scars. The conspiracy of compassion then begins as we allow God to breathe upon these wounds, revealing to us the promise that becomes a reality: We do not suffer alone. When we leave ourselves open to this promise even in our pain, we can inhale the breath of God.

Tracing our wounds is deeply personal and always painful. Each of us has experienced pain and suffering. If there is one thing we all know, it is our own pain, our own loss, our own sorrow. But it is precisely because we know it so well that God can be so present in our suffering. And the very fact that our own pain is so real is motivation enough to get involved in living the conspiracy of compassion.

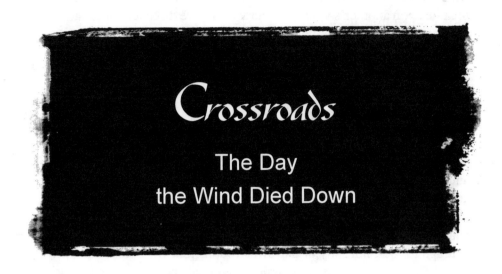

Crossroads

The Day
the Wind Died Down

Jesus is the paradigm for the breathing exercises that inspire us to be compassionate. The day of his expiration on the cross became the day of our inspiration to be a community of the cross. The breath of the resurrected Jesus makes his disciples co-conspirators to carry on the work of redemption. Because the wounds of crucifixion are still visible on the body of Christ, Jesus seems to be reminding his followers to never forget. Don't ever forget the day the wind of God died down and Jesus took his last breath.

Jesus' wounds teach his disciples that at the center of this conspiracy is the cross. The passion story of the Christian faith portrays this God of ours hanging in the balance between life and death. The picture is this: A young Jewish man is nailed to a cross planted on a hill outside of Jerusalem. He is naked and humiliated. A few fearful friends huddle nearby as the soldiers guarding the dying young man gamble to see who wins the only clothing he owns. The people who have come along to watch this spectacle laugh at the fallen savior's nakedness and all the promises he made that now seem so empty. Remember what he had said about destroying the temple and building it back up in only three days? "Where's your power now?" they shout. "You said you would save everybody else, save yourself! Come on, Jesus, show us your glory! Come down from that cross if you can!"

But Jesus stays on the cross. He endures the taunts and jeers, the rants and raves. Here we see the absolute aloneness of Jesus. He is abandoned by most of his followers, and everyone else ridicules him. They strip him of his power and possessions, his freedom and his friends, his dignity and his dreams. Jesus is silent in his suffering, save for the prayer of abandonment from Psalm 22: "My God, my God, why have you forsaken me?"

On the cross, Jesus experiences the true measure of isolation that suffering imposes on people. Stripped of everything from clothes to consolation, Jesus experiences loss completely — finally, the loss of his life. Even as his last breath ebbs away, Jesus breathes into his pain, even into the suffering beyond solace. As the skies darken, the thunder rolls and the lightning splits the heavens, Jesus screams in agony. His head falls to his chest. Death has claimed another victim.

During this excruciating ordeal, the cross becomes Christ's throne from which he ushers in a new kingdom. But there is no golden crown for the one who rules this reign; instead his captors weave a crown of thorns and violently push it down upon his head. There are no royal robes for the ruler of this reign; instead he stands naked before his tormentors who fall before him in mock adoration. There are no trumpet blasts to announce this reign; instead the sound of hammers pounding nails that tear through his flesh echo in the afternoon breeze. There is no vintage wine to celebrate the coronation of this king and the coming of this reign upon the earth; only vinegar to burn his bloody lips.

As the taunts and jeers increase, a thief on his left plays court jester to this king by mocking him and saying how he made the lame dance, the dumb sing, the blind see and the dead come back to life. He asks Jesus why he doesn't save himself now. But Jesus remains silent — a silence that resounds like thunder.

Jesus had been guilty of crimes of compassion. He had lived and laughed and loved, wept and mourned and suffered and shared; he had healed and harbored within his heart the hope of life. For these crimes of loving too much — and challenging others to live in kind — he is now being executed.

But before he dies, his last breath on earth will be the first breath of a new creation. As Jesus exhales, the other thief who has come to his defense, will inhale eternal life. For his faith, his insight into the suffering of Jesus and what it all means, this thief, this convicted felon, is given a future: "Today you will be with me in paradise." The good thief dares to take advantage of the moment of their common torture. This thief, the seed of faith exploding in his heart as he hangs from the gallows, inherits the wind of the Spirit and the reign of God.

The Paradox of the Cross

Too often we sanitize and sterilize the cross and fail to see it for what it was: a brutal instrument of torture and execution. Crucifixion was the most cruel form of capital punishment. On Calvary, we are confronted with the gruesome reality of crucifixion. Calvary is Christ's throne room, and there is nothing cozy or comfortable or compromising about the cross. Only when we see the cross for what it was can we embrace what it has become: an instrument of unconditional love on which God plays the song of life.

This paradox is captured perfectly in a simple story:

One evening a little girl was sitting on her mother's lap, listening to a fairy tale she had heard before. Her gaze drifted down from the book to her mother's arms. Looking up into her mother's eyes, she said, "Mommy, you have a beautiful face and beautiful eyes and beautiful hair. Why are your arms so ugly?"

The mother looked at her daughter with tenderness and gently closed the book of make-believe to tell her daughter the story behind her ugly arms.

"When you were a baby," she began softly, "I left you sleeping alone in your crib one evening. It was the first time I had ever left you alone in the house. I went down the street to a neighbor's for just a few minutes, but while I was gone, our house caught on fire. When I realized it was our house burning, I raced up the street. I dashed through the flames and grabbed you out of your crib. As I moved through the smoke and flames, I held you close to me, trying to protect you from the fire with my hands and arms. As I ran with you to safety, my hands and arms were badly burned. That's why they are so ugly."

With tears in her eyes, the little girl looked at her mother and said, "Mommy, you have a beautiful face and eyes and hair. But your hands and arms are the most beautiful of all."

The mother risked her life that her daughter might live, and her hands and arms bore the scars of her crucifixion. Jesus gave his life so that we might live, and he showed the disciples his hands and side so that they might believe. And so, ugliness becomes beauty; the cross becomes life.

The experience of Jesus on the cross has been described as "the labor pains of God's new birth." We see this new birth erupt in the moment of Jesus' death when the curtain of the temple was ripped to shreds, the earth shook and one of soldiers guarding the cross announced, "Truly this man was the Son of God" (Mk. 15: 39). It is in his death, in his complete abandonment and aloneness, in his surrender to God's will, that Jesus is revealed as the one who gives his life for others. Like the good thief, the centurion's profession of faith upon seeing the way Jesus died acknowledges and affirms the birth of hope. Jesus' last breath was the centurion's first breath of faith.

Jesus loved even in the suffering. He called others to life even as he hung from his instrument of torture, his cross. He built our future out of the wood of his cross. From the ashes of a dream, he stirred into flame newfound faith.

Community of the Cross

There is no suffering, no cross we bear, which does not resemble the cross of Christ. The challenge of our conspiracy is to become, with the good thief, with the centurion who came to believe after witnessing Jesus' death, and with those few friends huddled near Calvary, a community of the cross. How does one accept this challenge? How does one find the courage to crowd around the cross when most everyone else has taken flight? How does one stay close to the suffering when the temptation is to turn and run away? The answers to these questions are found in our willingness to touch, maybe even kiss, the wood of our own cross.

When I was in my twenties and on leave from my studies in the seminary, I lived in midtown Kansas City and worked at the diocesan newspaper. In the neighborhood where I lived there was a man who would sit in his wheelchair on the corner of a busy intersection. I saw him every morning when I went to work and he prepared for his daily routine of earning enough money to buy his next meal.

I never learned his name because I often walked the other way.

The wheelchair was his way around his world, a domain not much larger than that midtown intersection. A drugstore, a bookstore, an organic food store and an all-night cafe were the four corners of his globe. His hands were raw from traveling.

I remember one day when I was walking back from the grocery store waiting for the light to change. There he sat in his sacred space, the smell of his dirty clothes filling the air with an odor of decay. An empty Coke can without a top was tied to the arm of his chair. I dropped a couple of coins into the can and followed the traffic light's command: WALK.

If he made enough money during the morning shift, he would go across the street to the drugstore for lunch. One day when I happened to be in the store, I heard him order a tuna salad sandwich and a cup of coffee to wash it down. The girl behind the counter was pleasant but she didn't know his name either. She had another customer to wait on — one that could sit on a stool at the counter. The man ate his sandwich slowly. With no clock to punch, no appointments to keep, he savored every bite. Besides, he didn't know how generous the afternoon crowd would be.

I saw him almost every day I lived in the area, but I never saw him smile. His life was hard and smiles were for people without any pain.

When he finished his lunch that day, he pushed himself through the narrow aisle (the store was definitely designed for people with legs, not wheels). He bumped into a display of back-to-school items, and packages of pencils tumbled to the floor. Everyone turned to see who had been so clumsy. But our eyes were fixed just for an instant on the figure in the rusty chair with pencils on his lap. Then we turned away as if we had not heard the noise. If we didn't hear, we didn't have to help.

When the heat of the day became too much for him, he would visit the bookstore because it was air-conditioned.

If his can clinked enough during the afternoon, he ate dinner at the all-night cafe. If not, he would hope tomorrow would be better for change. He was experienced enough to know that silent collections were for cathedrals, not street corners.

When I moved back to the city some years ago, I went to that intersection in midtown to see if he was still around. But there was no sign of the forlorn figure in the rusty wheelchair. Funny, though, that after all these years I find his face among the cluttered photographs of people without names I have passed along the way.

This man in the rusty wheelchair knew the meaning of suffering. He could have been a mentor to me in learning about compassion if I had been an interested student at the time. But I was in a hurry, as I often am, and missed the opportunity to learn from him. Admittedly, entering his world would have been tentative at best. After all, I was young. I could walk and run. I had a few dollars in the bank and didn't have to depend on the kindness of strangers for my survival. But I could have stopped now and then and maybe tried to let him teach me about his world — and allow his world to touch mine if only for a brief time.

I wasn't ready then. Even though the reason I was living there at the time was the result of an experience of betrayal that called into question my belief in community and the meaning of friendship, I was too self-absorbed in my own pain and confusion to be aware of anyone else's. Though I felt the weight of this betrayal crushing me, I wasn't ready to embrace the suffering it brought, let alone kiss its cross. I was trying to extricate myself from beneath the betrayal and to run as far away from it as I could, lest the weight of its cross might push me deeper into the mystery of suffering.

Though this man's plight moved me on the surface, it did not move me to compassion but only to commiseration. I felt sorry for him. Perhaps the leap from commiseration to compassion comes out of a willingness to embrace one's own cross first. In carrying the weight of one's own cross, in solidarity with the one who carried the great cross, one finds an inner strength to help another carry his or her cross. The few coins I dropped into the man's cup were a sign of my sympathy, not an act of empathy. I did not as yet see this person as part of my circle of community. My circle was much smaller then as I struggled with trying to find some kind of meaning in my own sorrow.

There is a ritual in the Roman Catholic tradition on Good Friday that conveys eloquently this need to embrace the crosses of our lives before we can move with compassion to help another in need. It is called the *Veneration of the Cross.* All who come to remember the death of Jesus are invited to kiss the crucifix. In doing so, people are encouraged to bring to the cross their own suffering, pain and loss. With this one kiss, this gentle, intimate gesture of love, each person seeks to unite his or her own suffering with the suffering of Jesus. This kiss reflects an intimacy and a solidarity in the experience of suffering. This simple, sacred gesture helps one to recognize the presence of sorrow in one's life while also awakening a desire to unite one's agony with the suffering of others. In solidarity with others and with our suffering savior, the passion to act with compassion takes root in us.

But remember: Kissing the cross will leave a bad taste in one's mouth. It is the taste of ashes. The wood of the cross is charred by what we suffer. This old, rugged cross has caught fire and is fueled when dreams are consumed, when hopes go up in smoke, when love becomes but a faint ember glowing in the darkness.

A Spirituality of Ashes

I did not respond with compassion to that man in the wheelchair because I had not wanted to taste the ashes of my burned-out dream. I was unwilling to roll around in ashes. After the betrayal that led to my departure from the seminary, I just wanted to dust myself off and start a new life. More than anything, I wanted to forget the past and get on with my life.

If we image the cross as a door to a deeper life, then compassion is the key. But to find that key, we must be willing from time to time to roll around in our own ashes. For the key is buried beneath the ashes of our own personal story. A parable may help illustrate what I mean.

Imagine you are walking down the street and come upon a house that has burned to the ground. Sitting in the midst of the ashes and rubble is a man in his mid-thirties. The young man, a professional, who might otherwise be a striking symbol of sanity and success, is rubbing the ashes on his arms, his shirt, his trousers.

You stop on the sidewalk to watch him. At first you think the fire which destroyed the house also took his mind. One of his neighbors is standing beside you and tells you that this is the house where this young man lived as a child. The house had been vacant for a couple years since the death of the young man's grandfather.

"He was looking to sell the house," the neighbor says, "but he never got around to it." Then he adds, "Come to think of it, I don't think he ever came to take care of his grandfather's possessions after he died. He's busy, you know, with his career and all."

Now it is too late. All that is left is ashes.

The young man stands and then stumbles over charred beams and scarred remains. You want to step forward to comfort him but can't. What if he has indeed gone insane? No telling what he might do. You watch and whisper with the others.

But wait, he's found something. The young man picks up a tiny object and holds it in his hand. He brushes away the powdery ash and rubs it on his face. Now his bath is complete. He is covered with ashes.

You inch closer to see what it is the young man has found. Whatever it is, it's not very large. His hands hide it. Perhaps it is an heirloom of some sort. Then you see the tarnished chain that slips through his fingers. A watch dangles at the end of the chain. Gracefully, gently, it glides back and forth as the young man gazes, hypnotized by memory.

You hear him say softly, "This was my grandfather's. Just before he died, he gave it to me." It is one of those pocket watches you put in your vest. The young man opens it and a smile slightly creases his face.

He puts the watch in his pocket and falls back to the ground. A cloud of dust rises as the young man rolls around in the ashes of the place he once called home.

"He's lost his mind," the neighbor whispers.

No, you think to yourself, he's found his soul.

The conspiracy of compassion invites us to roll around in our ashes as the wind of God causes them to stir and swirl and surround us. In the tradition of the church, the season of Lent is the season of ashes, of repentance. We begin by having a tiny cross of ashes etched on our foreheads. They remind us of the dreams we have had that have turned to dust, of the life inside us that has died because of sin, of the hopes that have been consumed by despair, of the peace lost in pride and prejudice.

How foolish these ashes look clinging to our foreheads. How silly we look walking around with dirty faces. How humble and human we feel as someone politely points out, "You have something on your forehead."

More than a simple ritual of remembering that "We are dust and unto dust we shall return," receiving ashes is a sacred act of courage. It says: Yes, I am willing to wrestle in the darkness of these days where the shadows of sin play hide and seek, where clouds of indifference have eroded commitment, where cold winds of compromise have chilled compassion.

Ashes say: Yes, I am willing to confront those death-dealing attitudes and death-defying actions that have become second nature to me. Yes, I am willing to roll around in the ashes of my life as an act of repentance and remembering.

Even when I wash my face, the ashes cling. They remind me that I will work with God to bring new life out of those ashes, new life out of me.

This is the only way it can be done, the only way new life can emerge.

One reason we see so much indifference toward the suffering and pain of others is because we are afraid to look closely at our own pain and suffering. The reason we allow wars to rage, bombs to burst and bodies to burn is that we have failed to wash our hearts and hands, our minds and souls in our own ashes. For when we do, those ashes cling to us and leave fingerprints on everything and everyone we touch. Yet when we tear open our hearts, we allow God to get inside and God's fingerprints are left behind.

But, again, to feel such Godprints we must be willing to roll around in the ashes of our lives. We must be willing to play in them, pray with them, and only then profit from them. Only by rolling around in our own ashes will we reverence the ashes of others; respect their pain; see their anguish; embrace their wound.

Only by rolling around in our ashes will we find the key of compassion hidden there. Just as that young man found his grandfather's watch, we will find compassion. By rummaging through the rubble together, we will find our common identity as children of God. By stirring these ashes, we will spark a flame that will become a gift of love for another.

We realize, of course, that if we are faithful to this practice of ashes, people may think we have lost our minds. After all, playing in ashes is acting contrary to what the world so easily turns its back on: ashes, death and destruction. A good example of this attitude of denial was the euphoria in the United States following the war in the Persian Gulf. Some, including the president, said the "victory" in the gulf finally put "Vietnam behind us." Vietnam, of course, was the war the United States "lost"; or at least failed to achieve a military victory. Vietnam was the war that scarred both individuals and the nation. It divided the country in a way no conflict had since the Civil War. But when Saddam Hussein's aggression was crushed in the Persian Gulf, the military might of the United States was once again viewed as superior. Yet when all the parades were finished, the problems in the country's soul persisted. The scars of those soldiers who served in Vietnam survived. The pain of those families that lost loved ones in Vietnam was not assuaged by the rhetoric that the United States had "won" the war in the Persian Gulf.

When we have amnesia about the ashes of our lives, it's easier to accept war and violence and poverty as the way the world is: the expected results of a fallen world. Original sin becomes less original as we see the sins of genocide inflicted upon succeeding generations. Though the survivors of the Holocaust warned us consistently, prophetically and powerfully never to forget, amnesia soon settled in the world's soul and brought us Cambodia, Bosnia and Rwanda. A culture steeped in denial about death easily slips into complacency about life. We may feel sorry for those who experience the wounds of war. We may shake our heads in sorrow as we see the victims of violence. We may be moved to sympathize with the plight of the poor. But these attitudes place us in a position of accepting death as a way of life rather that seeing our way through death to a new way of living. When we are in touch with our own ashes, taste the bitterness of our own experiences of death, we begin to sense that there is another way of living and being in the world.

By remembering and reverencing our own ashes, we begin the movement from the isolation suffering imposes to solidarity with all those who suffer. And when enough people individually and corporately breathe into their wounds, when they know their pain, know what they have suffered and commit themselves to never forget, they begin to breathe together to lift the veil that shrouds the face of death.

The conspiracy of compassion is about losing our minds that divide us and rending hearts that confine us as we stumble over the charred remains of dusty dreams, broken peace and scarred hopes. It is about losing minds that accept the winds of war, violence and poverty as barometers and finding souls, scarred and covered with ashes, weary of war and tired of death, who breathe together to change the direction of the wind.

This breathing together, then, becomes the crosswinds that blow across the landscape littered with losses, crowded with crosses, scattered with the sacred bones of the dead that resurrect the memory of Ezekiel: "From the four winds come, O Spirit, and breathe into these slain that they may come to life" (Ez. 37: 9).

No, we don't have the answers for all the world's ills, evils and dis-eases. But if we have the courage to live the questions in solidarity with others and are faithful to the quest, then we may discover how the Spirit of God breathing within us gives us the courage to change from self-centered ways into a growing respect for the needs of others. The Spirit loosens the grip that original sin and unoriginal indifference hold on our lives and frees us to remember what we must never forget: We are people of this conspiracy not because of any merit of our own but because we have been called by God, because God's fingerprints are felt on our wounds, because God's life breathes deep within us. It is because of God's mercy that we can be merciful. It is because of God's fidelity that we can be faithful. It is because of God's memory that we can be compassionate.

The Attitude of Compassion

Though discipleship is a matter of response — of seeing the face of God in every person we meet in the course of our lives — it starts in our own experience with the recognition of our own brokenness. Only then can we see the brokenness of others. When we begin to see how all human life, indeed all of creation, is interconnected, we sense the breeze stirring in our souls.

The whole idea of compassion is that God meets us where we are, meets us not with answers, but with God's very self. For Christians, the Incarnation means that God became human to share our pain and make it God's own. We take this fact of our faith so much for granted until we miss the opportunity to meet another in his or her pain. Like that nameless man in the wheelchair, we pass each other by every day and often fail to notice one another until that one day we are awakened to the absence of the other. Where is she? Where did he go? And for some strange reason, we feel alone.

In the conspiracy of compassion, we unite ourselves with the suffering and loss of others in the same way Jesus did. But this is precisely why our involvement in the conspiracy is so difficult. We are tempted to want instant answers or miracle cures. But as one looks at Jesus strapped to the cross, slowly suffocating as he hangs in the balance between life and death, one begins to see that there are no easy answers or cures or avenues of escape. There is only this one who is willing to take upon himself, in his body and in his soul, the suffering of others, the suffering of the world. Here Jesus is seen as being totally present to all the pain the world has to offer. This is his passion. The passion in Jesus' life is to save the world, and he seems to realize that unless one is willing to experience pain, one will never find one's true passion.

We find our true passion, and live *with* passion (which is the meaning of *com*passion) when we know for whom or for what we are willing to suffer. And yet we recognize that a willingness to suffer goes against a culture that tries to avoid suffering at all costs. Remedies and painkillers are within arm's reach. We want something or someone to take the pain away. Our God, however, chose not to take our pain away but to embrace our pain as God's own in the suffering and death of Jesus. By doing so, our God stands in solidarity with those who suffer in every age.

Paul describes this attitude in the great Philippians hymn when he writes that even though Jesus was "in the form of God," he did not grasp for divinity but rather "emptied himself, taking the form of a servant, being born in the likeness of (human beings)" (Phil. 2: 6-7). This attitude of Christ, Paul tells us, must be our attitude as well. It is an attitude of humility, of openness, of obedience, of compassion: "And being found in human form he humbled himself and became obedient unto death, even death on a cross" (Phil 2: 8).

When we seek to live in the mystery of suffering and walk the way of compassion, we often find ourselves standing at the crossroads of decision: Either we follow the path of compassion marked by the signs of faith and forgiveness, hope and hospitality, tenderness and trust; or we follow the path of indifference marked by greed and guilt, fear and the failure to reach out to others, selfishness and sin. The first leads to the destination of the cross and the community the cross conceives; the second, to alienation and the isolation apathy ultimately imposes.

An Identity Crisis

Our conspiring together confronts us with a question of identity. Each of us must name the pain of our lives. When Jesus invites us to take up our cross and follow in his footsteps, we must first recognize who we are. What gifts do we have to offer? What wounds do we have to give in the service of others?

We often see gifts as skills or talents we possess. Perhaps we might look at our gifts more as expressions of the Spirit. The gifts of the Spirit, like wisdom and understanding, are gifts gained from experience. We are shaped and gifted by the experiences of our lives. These gifts of experience express the movement of the Spirit in our lives and lend themselves to creating an attitude of compassion as we learn from these experiences. We gain wisdom from being open to the wounds we have suffered. We learn understanding from standing under and breathing into our own pain.

Though it is difficult, perhaps impossible, to view the wounds we have endured as gifts, wounds will, through time and the discipline of leaving them exposed, teach us a way to serve. Recall the woman and her husband whose son was killed by a drunk driver. This incurable wound remained open and offered them a way to serve my family and me the morning after my brother committed suicide. Though they could have chosen to become bitter and angry over the loss of their son, instead they chose to allow their wound to move them to compassion by serving those who were experiencing grief and loss.

This question of identity raised by our gifts and our wounds must have been on Jesus' mind that day when he asked his disciples, "Who do the people say that I am?" (Lk. 9: 18). He was probably not interested in his press clippings or what the commentators on the "Good News Network" were saying about his latest revival. Instead, Jesus wanted to elicit from his disciples what was stirring within them. Some stayed on the surface and repeated only what the headlines were reporting: *Has John the Baptist Come Back as a Carpenter from Nazareth?* or *Elijah Returns to Earth, Search Is on for Chariot* or *Prophet of Old Sends New Signal.*

So Jesus focused his query, "But who do you say that I am?" Peter, often the first to speak and so often afflicted with foot-in-mouth syndrome, this time reached beneath the surface and removed his sandal long enough to say, "The Christ of God" (Lk. 9: 20).

What follows, of course, is the litany of implications about his identity as Messiah: "The Son of Man must suffer many things, and be rejected by the elders and chief priests and scribes, and be killed..." (Lk. 9: 22). That must have startled the disciples. After all, the Messiah they had been taught to expect was one that would come with great power and glory — perhaps a strong military person who would lead the forces of resistance against the oppressive enemy. Now here was Jesus telling them that the Messiah finds his strength in weakness, his glory in suffering, his life in death.

If we want to think of ourselves as co-conspirators, this little treatise by Jesus on his true identity should shake us and startle us too. Because when Jesus identified himself as a suffering Messiah, he also implicated us. Our identity as children of God and followers of Christ means — like that mother saving her daughter from the fire — that we are to live our lives for others. It implies a willingness to suffer with and for others. It calls us to help others carry the burdens, the crosses, the losses, of their lives.

We can do this when we have taken that first step and named our own pain. It is precisely because I have felt my own pain that I recognize my identity as a person who has something to give to another: the gift of my own experience. Rather than nursing my own wound to the exclusion of everyone else, I allow it to be the author of my compassion for others.

This is the salvation strategy outlined by Jesus in his suffering Messiah sermon: Losing our lives in love for another leads to liberation. We are free to lose ourselves precisely because we have first found ourselves. We know who we are. In assessing our gifts and our wounds, we accept our identity as people who are, beyond all the labels we may use to describe or define ourselves, the beloved of God. When we know who we are as God's beloved, we have nothing to lose and everything to gain. As Janis Joplin sang in the early 1970s, "Freedom's just another word for nothing left to lose." So our liberation to be compassionate comes from the knowledge that we belong to God, not ourselves, and so there's "nothing to lose"; we are free to love as God loves.

What we gain from this losing is not only the wisdom and

knowledge that we are God's beloved, but also a community of wounded and wonderful women and men who have gone through this same process of losing and so have found themselves. In this companionship of sacred souls, we come to the unshakable calm, the unmovable center, the unambiguous knowledge that we are not alone.

As the cross loomed large in Jesus' losing, so it is for us. It is a losing that can mean many things, but at its core means taking the risk to name our own pain so that we might be present to another's anguish. I don't know the crosses you carry. I only know this: Two can carry a cross easier than one. Just ask Jesus. Simon of Cyrene was forced out of the crowd, no longer to be a spectator, a long-necked curiosity-seeker, but to become a participant, a strong-shouldered faith-finder.

No one wants to suffer. Everything being equal, we would probably like to stay on the sidelines, serenely detached like Simon, content to watch the events that pass before us. We spend much of our lives avoiding pain, taking extra-strength Tylenol when regular strength is not enough to numb the sudden realization that we are not immune. The agents of advertising tell us we don't have time for the pain. But Jesus reminds us that suffering is part of life; indeed, it is a part of our identity. And rather than seeking avenues of escape, Jesus invites us to enter the fray. Not because suffering is good or pain is grand, but because, believe it or not, we can do something about it. We can allow God to redeem it.

This is the challenge of our conspiracy, our breathing together in communion with God and with all of creation. It may seem unrealistic, perhaps unimaginable. When it does, we often place those values that seem out of sync with society high on a shelf labeled *idealism*. There they remain, out of reach. Every now and then, though, someone comes along to remove them, dust them off and show us how they are possible. Just as that little girl learned the central tenet of our faith in her mother's scarred arms, so each of us has been touched at one time or another by people of faith who have passed on to us, either in words or deeds, the breath of new possibility. Each one of us knows someone who has given us a holy kiss that sparks a flame buried beneath the ashes inside, a person who resuscitates a dream left for dead.

I count myself blessed to have received this gift from many, but one person in particular comes to mind: Gram.

Dancing with the Cross

My maternal grandmother was a woman full of life and vitality. She spent her life as a farmer, a lover of the land. Gram awoke early each morning and went about her simple but necessary daily tasks with quiet dedication. A strong woman, though slight of build, Gram was committed to her way of life and demanded the same kind of commitment from her children and grandchildren in whatever walk of life we pursued.

I loved visiting Gram and staying with her during the summer vacations of my youth. Being from the city, the farm was a special place to spend some of my best summers — playing baseball with my cousins; baling hay in the hot summer sun; feeding the cows and calves; helping out in the milking pit.

But as the years passed, a subtle but noticeable change came over Gram. The weight of the years made her once-strong back to bend. Her legs ground to a halt. Her fingers became stiff and swollen. Arthritis had invaded her body and left her strong and sturdy bones brittle and dry.

She walked with a cane for awhile and then used a walker. It wasn't long before a wheelchair became the only way Gram could move around her world. Then, when every move she made was accompanied by pain, the nursing home and professional care seemed like the only alternative.

At this point it appeared to us that Gram had lost her will to live. She had enjoyed a full and beautiful life, but the loss of her limbs and the immobility of her bones seemed to render her once-active life useless. Appearing weary of life, Gram died about a year after she went to the nursing home.

What strikes me most about Gram's story is that throughout her crippling ordeal, she did not blame God or feel as if God had played a cruel cosmic trick on her. Even though she could no longer do those wonderful, simple things — like feed the chickens or bake homemade bread that smelled like heaven or make apple butter in a big, black cauldron on those cold, gray October afternoons — she kept her faith. In fact, I am convinced that in those last few years she grew to know God even more deeply. In her weakness, in abandoning all those things she had been busy about all her life, in coming to terms with her own pain, she was filled with God's loving presence in a way she had never known before.

In her weariness, with her tired, dry and aching bones, Gram was found by God. And so she didn't give up or lose her will to live. Quite the contrary was true. Gram had moved to a level of love with God that few of us experience because we are afraid to let go. Gram exhaled all her worry and wondering and breathed in God's spirit of peace. Taking up her cross, Gram walked with God out of the valley of dry bones to the mountain of fresh hope.

What to us looked like a bed of pain worthy of our pity was to Gram a bed of rest in the palm of God.

To me Gram's life and death capture what Jesus means when he says, "Deny your very self, take up your cross and follow in my steps" (Mk. 8: 34). Gram followed the steps taught to her by Jesus and found life. With her arthritic knees and aching feet, Gram learned to dance to the music of God's love played on the instrument of salvation, the cross. She danced her way into heaven with the cross of life on her back. In doing so, she tried to teach me how to dance. The steps flow from these lyrics to the music: "Whoever loses her life for my sake will save it."

I'm still learning how to dance and I think I know why. At weddings or receptions or family gatherings where people got out on the dance floor, I would usually decline by saying, "Thanks, anyway, but I don't know how to dance." Well, if truth be told, it was not that I did not know how; it was because I was afraid. I was too self-conscious about how I would look trying to dance.

When we are too self-conscious, we can't dance.

Dancing frees the body and unleashes the spirit. We move in motion with another to the sound of music. We forget about how we look and look instead into the eyes of the other. By following in the dance steps of Jesus, we are led out of ourselves and into God.

But it takes practice. It is like the figure skaters we watch on television. They appear so graceful and so fluid in their motion. They are beautiful to watch, but I must admit I get nervous. I don't want to see them fall. When they do one of those triple-axles and leap in the air, I cringe because I just know they will miss their landing and fall flat on the ice. But if they were afraid of falling, they would never get out on the ice. They have to forget about themselves and their fears and just skate to the music. Forget about the crowd and focus only on the dance.

The breath of Jesus, filled with peace and promise, beckons us to make fear a forgotten friend and step out on the ice. The body of Jesus, bruised but not broken, bridges the chasm of what might have been, and what is yet to come, with new possibility. The Spirit of Jesus draws us together in a conspiracy of compassion as we lose ourselves in the dance of life.

The Mystery of Suffering

It is never easy to name the pain of our lives and our world. There are realities of suffering that are beyond our reach of understanding. They seep deep beneath the surface and find their roots in the mysteries of life and death. Those mysterious realities find their home only in the heart of God and the paschal mystery.

In the same way we seek to unravel the mystery of suffering, we seek to explore the nature of compassion. It too is a mystery that must be lived. We breathe deeply into the mystery, not seeking to solve it but to live within it. We breathe in and out, sometimes inhaling some fresh air of hope while exhaling some sorrow. But we keep breathing because to breathe is to live. Compassion is an attitude that finds its meaning in this simple act of breathing, of being, in the heart of mystery.

When we hear that word *mystery,* our first inclination might be to think of an Agatha Christie novel or Jessica Fletcher on *Murder, She Wrote.* Television has given us the impression that mysteries can be solved in an hour, including commercials. Or we might think of mystery as the answer we received in high school religion classes to questions that had no answer. Remember asking the teacher to explain the Trinity and hearing, "It's a mystery"?

Unlike television dramas that seek to solve mysteries within a fixed time frame, suffering is a mystery precisely because there are no answers. There are some problems that cannot be fixed. There is some pain where there is no relief. There are some illnesses that have no cure. There are some experiences that are beyond our understanding. How can one explain the demonic brutality of a Hitler, a Stalin or the Khmer Rhouge in Cambodia? We wonder how to respond to the "ethnic cleansing" in the former Yugoslavia or the genocide in Rwanda that repulsed and yet baffled everyone from politicians to the pope. How do we stop it? Do we "fix" it by force or by humanitarian aid? No one doubts the desire to end the suffering, but what can we do?

What answers do we give to random acts of violence? A young man is sitting in his car in the parking lot of a local nightspot. Three youths approach him, ask for money and then shoot him in the head. We hear the story on the news or read about it in the morning paper. But unless that young man is a relative, a friend or a classmate of our own child, the tragic event usually becomes just another example of how corrupt and evil our present age has become. We turn the page or switch the channel and look for some good news for a change.

But when that murdered young man is someone we know, someone we love, suddenly the pain and hurt is almost too much to bear. We begin searching for clues but find little consolation. We struggle to understand how this could happen. Why is there so much evil in the world? In my world? We are confronted with the gnawing question, "Why?" We even call into question our faith: "Where is God in all of this? Where are you God?"

These are the questions that fill the air when suffering surrounds us and tragedy chokes our best attempts to catch our breath. How do we answer these inquiries into the unknown? When we encounter the scarred face of violence, how do we respond? When our faith is tested by forces of mayhem and madness beyond our control, when we hear about a tragedy that causes us to pause and size up our faith, what do we do?

First, we have the courage to ask the questions. We place them in the center of our breathing, our prayer. From experience, we know that when we pray in these situations of extreme suffering we pray not so much because we think our prayers will have an effect on the problems and pain of our world but because prayer affects the way we look at those problems, at that pain. The prayer of the one who seeks a compassionate heart refutes the cliche "Seeing is believing" with the conviction that we have to believe before we can see our way through pain and loss, suffering and despair. This quality of faith allows us to see in ways the world cannot see; it affords us the courage to trust in the vision even when the evidence seems to blur the vision of the reign of God beyond recognition.

This first step into the mystery of suffering is tentative at best. But being compassionate means we are willing to enter the fray of human suffering just as our God did. To be as compassionate as our God means we are willing to live these moments of anguish — moments that can be stretched into lifetimes — as fully as possible.

Pope Paul VI once defined mystery as "reality imbued with the hidden presence of God." The mystery of compassion begins to unravel in the image of God dying on the gallows of Calvary. This image which Christians have hanging in their churches and offices and bedrooms has the power to transform our lives. The cross has the power to turn death inside out and to flip our expectations of death — and life — upside down.

The image and reality of a God who suffers and dies means so much more than death and despair. It offers us a hope that transcends time and reaches to eternity. There is always hope for us if we are able to ask the questions, "Where is God?" and "Why, God?" because in those questions we find some breathing room to believe in a God who is present to us even in those moments when suffering seeks to suffocate us.

As people seeking the way of compassion, we have all found ourselves at that rest stop where we wonder why "bad things happen to good people." But perhaps that's the wrong question. Perhaps the better question is how we will allow this experience of suffering to shape us into a community of the cross. This is the question that will keep our sometimes fragile and fearful hearts open so that our true destiny as dreamers of God's reign might filter in and take root deeply in our heartland. This is the question that suggests we believe that all suffering splits the heart in two and allows our God an opening to come on through. When we keep those jagged lines in our cracked hearts open to the certainty that if not in our time but in God's time all will be one, we can find some real breathing space and so increase our capacity for compassion.

The Capacity for Compassion

Living in the mystery of suffering increases our lung capacity by focusing our breathing on the God who lives within us. When we experience inexplicable suffering either personally or on a cosmic scale, our image of God as the great power in the sky who keeps us safe and secure begins to shrink. The image of God that at one time afforded us a view through rose-colored windows of a world where everything was going to be all right now gets blurry and out of focus. Now, we look out the bloodstained windows of our soul to a world that is full of fear and so often caught in a vise of violence. And we believe in a God who is the great power within us. We believe in a God who gives us the courage to wake up every morning, to sit on our front porch and watch the neighborhood children play, to tell stories again to friends who stop by for a cup of coffee.

This is the God whose gift of faith we treasure, the gift that is guarded by the Holy Spirit living within us. This is the God who doesn't stay above the fray, distant and aloof, but who comes to dwell in the midst of our pain, our suffering, our sorrow in the person and spirit of Jesus. This is the God who, when we ask how long, whispers in our wounds and says, "the vision still has its time, pressed on to fulfillment, and will not disappoint." We may not see, but we do believe it. Believing it, we see a way to live by faith. And living it, we find our faith increasing, our love enlarging and our hope enduring.

When we breathe deeply, allowing God to restore life from within us, our capacity for compassion increases. When we grow in our capacity for compassion, we will be less prone to judge and more prepared to serve; more reluctant to condemn and more ready to console; more intent on decreasing the room in our hearts for fear even as we make more room for the infinitely spacious compassion of our God in Jesus Christ.

Ironically, when we increase our capacity for compassion, we make more room for joy. For when the gift of compassion is given to another, we discover that we receive so much more. Remember, the great Philippians' hymn does not end with Jesus hanging on the cross but rather concludes by singing how "God has highly exalted (Jesus) and bestowed on him the name which is above every name, that at the name of Jesus every knee should bow, in heaven and on earth and under the earth, and every tongue confess that Jesus Christ is Lord, to the glory of God" (Phil 2: 9-11).

If we are open to living this intense experience of the paschal mystery, we will likely discover a suffering not unlike that experienced by a young Jewish rabbi hanging on a cross outside the holy city of Jerusalem — a suffering that is unjustly imposed. Just as Jesus was unjustly condemned, so are countless others today: condemned to hunger and homelessness, to violence and oppression, to fear and loneliness. The compassion of Jesus speaks powerfully to this suffering not so much in words but in the eloquent witness of presence — the real presence of God in a world crying out for redemption.

In Jesus we see the wounds of our redemption. Our God believed that we were and are worth fighting for, not by using weapons of violence but the weapon of unconditional love: the cross.

In the mystery of suffering there are very few answers. But by breathing into the mystery, we will find our capacity for compassion. It will come in living the questions raised by our suffering not into answers but into acts of love.

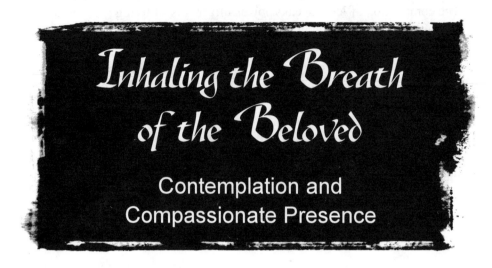

Inhaling the Breath of the Beloved

Contemplation and Compassionate Presence

The crosswinds that swirled on Calvary the day Jesus died crowned a life that was lived on the fringe. Throughout the Gospel portraits of Jesus, we find him hanging around those people of his day who had no connections. Here is where compassion and suffering meet and find their meaning. The conspiracy of Jesus was rooted in a willingness to suffer with others, even those no one else might find lovable. It was a willingness to experience the deepest hurts and longings of the human heart and embrace them as his own. His desire was to unite himself with others in the mystery of sorrow.

We see in Jesus how being compassionate runs in God's family. The prophet Hosea captured God's identity as a compassionate parent when he depicted Israel as a child loved by God (Hos. 11: 1, 3-4). Like a father who teaches his son how to walk and ride a bike, like a mother who nurses her daughter with comfort and holds her close to her face with tenderness, God desires such intimacy with us. God's arms become like "bands of love" that are elastic, giving us room to run freely, to fall and skin our egos. But those arms are always ready to draw us back close to God's breast.

The prophet Hosea reminded us that this is our basic identity: We are the beloved of God. This is who we are: God's beloved. But we tend to cover up this identity with so many labels that we forget who we are. For example, we identity ourselves with labels of relationship (mother, father, sister, brother, husband, wife, son, daughter, friend, acquaintance, enemy); labels of vocation (lawyer, nurse, teacher, plumber, priest, farmer, factory worker); labels of economic status (rich, poor, middle income family, homeless); political labels (liberal, conservative, moderate, right wing, left wing, centrist); religious labels (Protestant, Catholic, Buddhist, Hindu, Moslem); labels that describe our leaning within a particular denomination (fundamentalist, evangelical, traditionalist, progressive); labels of orientation (heterosexual, homosexual, bisexual). But beneath all these labels there is the truth that we share the same pedigree. We are, at the core of our being, all the beloved of God. When we strip away all the bumper stickers, we realize our identity in relation to God. When we peel away the scabs that scar our psyches, we come to know our Healer.

Hosea painted a beautiful picture of our Divine Healer who desperately wanted to be in relationship with a people who were wounded and broken. But being open to such an extraordinary relationship with God was too much for the people to comprehend. The prophet lamented that the people did not know that God was their healer. They are like so many of us who learn well the lessons of this world to be self-sufficient and so insulate ourselves from others, who hide behind labels or judge others by appearance, who seek fulfillment through the accumulation of possessions while divesting ourselves of depth, who stay on the surface and wonder where God has gone in our times of trouble.

But rather than feeling rejected at not being needed, God did not abandon the children. Instead, God's compassion grew even greater, deeper, wider and more tender.

Just as Hosea characterized God as a loving parent with a tender heart when God saw the people walking amid the chaos that had become their lives, we see the same emotion in Jesus when he saw the great crowds coming to him for healing. According to Matthew, "When he saw the crowds, he had compassion for them" (Mt. 9: 36). In the context of that passage, one reason the people were feeling so bent out of shape was because their religious leaders, the Pharisees, took everything so seriously. Jesus had just expelled a demon from a mute man and the crowds shouted his praise. But the Pharisees were more than skeptical, and some were downright cynical, accusing Jesus of using Satan's power to cast out the evil.

There was so much jealousy, so much dissension, so much pettiness and close-mindedness among these religious leaders who criticized Jesus' every move that the people were just worn out. There were so many broken, exhausted and wasted folks flocking to him that Jesus was moved to compassion. And his mission of compassion would not end until he shared with them their ultimate experience: death.

Jesus saw the killing fields of his day and realized there were few who would take the risks to go into those fields and harvest the pain with the promise of God. As we know from experience, it is risky to enter another's pain because we are entering the realm of mystery where words lose their meaning. We worry about what to say. We wonder how to strike the balance between not wanting to intrude if the person wants to be alone and yet wanting to stand ready if our presence is requested. But as we have also discovered, healing can only come from a heart that's been broken. We are compassionate precisely because we know what it means to be broken. Unlike the Pharisees in the Gospel who see something wrong even in an act of kindness, who see ulterior motives in every offer of help, co-conspirators in the compassion of Jesus are willing to take the risk and show others a care that flows from a heart that breathes even when it is broken.

In the killing fields of our day, the conspiracy of compassion calls us to be these laborers who are willing to walk through the fields of pain and with our presence to harvest hope. But our real presence in situations of suffering demands that we know who we are. Knowing our identity will shape our response. Since Jesus is the paradigm for our understanding of compassion as real presence in our own and another's suffering, we need to explore how Jesus came to recognize his identity as the incarnation of God's compassion.

Step Backwards into Solitude

In tracing the compassion of Jesus, we remember how he sought out solitary spaces in his life. Often this would follow times of intense healing, when calls for Jesus' compassion might stretch his heart thin.

The most dramatic example of Jesus seeking solitude is the story of his forty-day wilderness retreat before even beginning his public ministry. In Matthew's Gospel, Jesus goes to the desert to fast and pray immediately after his baptism by John in the Jordan. We recall that at the conclusion of his baptismal bath, a voice from the heavens splits the skies and thunders, "This is my beloved Son. My favor rests on him." With this identity as favorite son resting on his shoulders, Jesus embarks on a journey that will shape the rest of his ministry. Could it be he went into the wilderness to deepen his understanding of his identity and increase his capacity of compassion?

Hungry for God, thirsting for holiness in the desert, Jesus is tempted by the same forces that stifle compassion in us:

— by **power:** "Turn these stones into bread."
— by **fame:** "Throw yourself down from the temple."
— by **success:** "All these kingdoms will I bestow on you."

In response to these temptations, Jesus relies on a single defense: the Word of God. God's Word is the weapon that cuts through the alluring facade of power, fame and worldly success. Rather than giving in to the attractive promises of the present moment, Jesus gives his will to the enduring presence of God. He avoids the temptation to be a different kind of Messiah — one who could erase the pain and suffering of the world with the stroke of his hand, or a military ruler who could crush oppressors with an army of angels. It would be easy for Jesus to turn those stones into bread to show his power and feed his empty stomach. It would be so easy for Jesus to throw himself from the top of the temple, fly through the air with the greatest of ease and walk away unharmed and famous. It would be so easy for Jesus to win all the kingdoms of the world in a show of dazzling divinity. But he chooses instead to empty himself of such fragmentary and fleeting infatuations and to follow the way of the wilderness — the way of compassion.

The story of Jesus' wilderness retreat reminds us how dangerous the desert can be. To take off our shoes on the sacred, sandy soil of solitude is to act in defiance of a world that values power, fame, fortune and success more than anything else in this or any other world. When we enter the desert, we may never be the same again.

We go to the wilderness of solitude for the same reason Jesus went to the desert: to know who we are in relation to God and to others. We go to the desert not to escape people, but to learn how to love them. We go to the desert to deepen our identity as co-conspirators in God's plan of compassion. It is a great paradox that our awareness of the anguish of our neighbor across the world or across the street increases when we seek the sacred space of solitude. A retreat to solitude leads to solidarity with the suffering people of our planet. In solitude we embrace the suffering of Jesus Christ, the crucified one, the compassionate one who opens our eyes and unplugs our ears so that we might notice the one we passed by yesterday.

Making Real God's Presence

Illustrations of the effects this sojourn of solitude had on Jesus' ministry are numerous in Scriptures. For example, remember the day when Jesus comes upon a funeral procession in the city of Nain (Lk. 7: 11-17). Jesus notices the pain and anguish on the face of the widow of Nain, and because he notices, a son is given a new lease on life and a mother finds a future.

Remember the story: A young man has died. He was an only child and his mother is a widow. Jesus had never met the dead young man or his widowed mother, and yet "he had compassion on her and said to her, 'Do not weep.'" Jesus, because of his compassion at seeing the grief of the mother, raises the dead young man to life and "gives him to his mother."

This story holds a poignant place in my memory as I recall the time when I was in charge of my religious community's efforts to attract more vocations to the priesthood and religious life. One of my responsibilities was to publish a couple of newsletters that were sent out to young men who might be interested in the priesthood. Since I was also in charge of the seminarians who were in formation, I was only able to visit those on our mailing list who were strongly considering applying to our formation program and entering a more formal discernment process. So most of the young men on our vocation mailing list were only names to me.

One day the most recent newsletter I had mailed out was returned to me with a note from a young man's mother. Her words were very simple and etched in sorrow: "Please remove my son Jason's name from your mailing list; instead remember him in your prayers as he died this past year."

I called the pastor of the parish where Jason belonged and learned that Jason had committed suicide the summer before. I had never met him or his family. The pastor told me that Jason had lost his dad about ten years ago and that he had one brother who was in college.

Until his mother wrote me that note, Jason was just another name on the mailing list. A push of a button on the computer would fulfill his mother's request and remove his name. But like that old man's face who looked at me from his rusty wheelchair years before, I haven't been able to close out this account in my memory bank.

It was a strange feeling to receive a note telling me that someone I had never met was dead. Certainly the fact that he was so young contributed to the grief I felt for his mother. And the circumstances of his death — suicide — moved me to remember my own brother. I also thought of the pain Jason's mother must have felt those past few months receiving our newsletters in her son's name.

How I wanted to do for Jason's mother what Jesus did for the widow of Nain. We have no such power, but we can cultivate the fertile soil of our soul and see how the seeds of compassion begin to grow into courageous acts of love: to suffer with those who suffer, to mourn with those who mourn, to walk with those who are weary, to abide with those who are abandoned. Not that we can take their pain away or heal their wounds or bring their loved ones back to life, but rather to remind them by our presence, by our love, by our unspoken words, that they are not alone.

This is the truly important miracle that took place at Nain. It is not so much that Jesus raised the dead youth to life, because mortality is a given condition of humanity and at some point the man would die. The real miracle is that in the compassion of Jesus for the youth and his mother, those who saw it and experienced it were awakened to the reality of God's presence in their lives. The ones who witnessed this miracle proclaimed that "God has visited the people." It was the person of Jesus and his compassionate touch that allowed the people to praise God and say, "A great prophet has arisen among us."

This is how God visits the people of our earth even today: In ordinary and human ways that are charged with divine love we make God's presence known in our world. We do this by first embracing our identity as God's beloved. We do this by first understanding that we are known and loved by God. When we know who we are, we are more likely to trust our basic instincts that are revealed in our identity as God's beloved and notice those along the way whose silent screams or anguished expressions cry out for our compassion.

Contemplation and Compassion

Seeking out solitary spaces to contemplate the mysteries of life and how the Divine Mystery moves within us and all of creation captures a basic truth about who we are and who we are not. Often we look at solitude and the experience of contemplative prayer as a way of becoming holy. But perhaps the truth is that contemplation teaches us that we are not so much human beings trying to become holy as we are holy beings trying to become more human. Contemplation puts us in touch with this basic belief of our existence: that because God, in Jesus Christ, became human, our holiness lies in our humanness. It awakens us to the fact that we are God's beloved. Made in the image of God, we are holy. This is who we are: sons and daughters of the Most High.

The practice of contemplative prayer leads to compassionate presence. When we take the plunge into contemplation and taste our holiness, we sense the compassion of God as part of our image as God's children. Our holiness is played out in our being more human, in realizing our oneness with our sisters and brothers as a basis for forming a human, compassionate heart. From this posture of prayer that places us within the Divine Mystery, we take the leap to become a compassionate presence in the world. When we touch the holiness within, we respond by becoming more wholly human in all of our relationships.

To help explore this connection between contemplation and compassionate presence we draw upon two familiar stories from the Gospel of Luke: the Good Samaritan and the tale of the two sisters, Martha and Mary.

The Martha and Mary story reflects the need for a holy rhythm between work and relationships. It reminds us that this delicate balance must be maintained to sustain a creative energy. In a task-oriented world where the focus is often on the work that must be accomplished, it is so easy to overlook the necessity for relationships that nurture the soul, what Jesus calls in that Gospel tale, "the better part."

The story is told in the section of Luke's Gospel that recounts some of the events in Jesus' life as he makes his way to Jerusalem. Jesus has just answered the interrogation of the lawyer who wanted to know what he had to do to inherit everlasting life. Jesus replies by telling him to look at the law, which the lawyer knows by memory if not by heart. He has memorized the laws about loving God and loving neighbor. But his stumbling block to understanding concerns the notion of just who should be considered a neighbor.

Here is where Jesus launches into the story about the Good Samaritan, perhaps the most eloquent expression in the Scriptures of compassionate action.

As we are so well aware, it was the outcast, the enemy, who responded with compassion to the one who fell victim to the robbers. This parable clearly illustrates what Jesus says earlier in Matthew's Gospel about "loving your enemies" and "praying for those who persecute you." This Samaritan did more than pray for someone who was a member of the society that persecuted him. He acted with kindness toward the man who was supposed to be his enemy. Indeed, the same language that is used to describe Jesus' reaction to the suffering crowds is used to describe the Samaritan's emotions when he came upon the man left for dead by the side of the road: He was moved by compassion.

What motivated the Samaritan to get involved in the plight of this person victimized by thieves? What moved him to respond with such compassion? Perhaps the answer is found in the Samaritan's own experiences of suffering. Though we don't know the particulars of his pain, we do know that because of his identity as a Samaritan, he was an outcast. As one living outside the law, he would have been treated with disdain. He would have become accustomed to rejection. But rather than allowing his status as a "second-class citizen" to deter him from reaching out to one in need, he used his own experiences of suffering to motivate him to become involved, even though the one he was helping was a member of the group that persecuted him. There was nothing he could do about his status as a Samaritan — this was his heritage. But he understood that beneath this label of ancestry was his true identity as the beloved of God. This was his motivation: He knew who he was, and he knew what he had suffered.

Often when reflecting on this story, we focus on the so-called "holy ones" — the priest and Levite — who passed the victim without helping. Certainly their lack of response exhibits a lack of compassion. Or, at the very least, a lack of awareness of their own pain. They had not taken the time to feel their pain or to know their suffering. They were in a hurry to get to the temple. They couldn't take time for the pain. And, of course, because they were so confined by the laws of ritual purity, to stop and help this person would have made them unclean and unable to enter the temple to pray.

But the Samaritan, who in the minds of those listening to this story was not the man's neighbor, was the one who did the "neighborly" thing. He followed the trail of blood seeping out of the wounds of the one who had been robbed and beaten, and cared for him. He knew who he was. He knew what he had suffered. He was not constrained by ritual regulations or concerned about religious laws. Rather, he saw someone in need — someone like himself who had been pushed away from the center of community and left for dead at the side of the road — and so he stopped to help him.

To be a "neighbor" means to treat another with compassion. That is the moral of the story that is not missed by the lawyer who asked Jesus the initial question. We are told to follow the example of the Samaritan and treat others with the same quality of love and concern. But the problem is that we still tend to categorize groups into "friends" and "enemies," "neighbors" and "others."

The invitation of contemplation is to get beneath the labels to discover our true identity at the center of our being. When we allow the breath of God to blow like a gentle breeze over us and within us, the labels we so often use to define us and others are swept away. This letting go of the labels that confine us is part of the radical truth of discipleship, which when practiced is a clear sign of the in-breaking of the reign of God. Our world tends to define people by nationality, by race, by religious preference, by political ideology, by sexual orientation. We learn from early in life that the world is divided into these "neighborhoods." When we dare to go beyond these impulses and learned behaviors of the "world," then we are living in the "reign."

Activism Activated by Contemplation

As Jesus leaves the lawyer to ponder the parable of the Good Samaritan and what it means to be neighbor, he enters a village where Martha welcomes him to her home.

Traditionally, Martha and Mary have been seen as symbols of the apostolic and contemplative lifestyles. And since Jesus praises Mary, the contemplative one, we assume that contemplation is "the better part." But what exactly is *the better part*? Remember the story. Notice Mary's stance: She is sitting below Jesus, humbly listening to his words. Martha, on the other hand, is standing above Jesus, scurrying about the house "distracted by her many tasks." Mary focuses all her attention on Jesus. Martha, on the other hand, is so busy that she doesn't realize all her distractions are really secondary to the primary purpose of discipleship: Love the God who sits in our living room. Love the God who tells stories of solidarity. Love the God who is right here, right now. Love the God who desires to be in communion with us if only we allow all the distractions to dissipate.

Though Martha welcomes Jesus to her home and is busy about all the details of hospitality, it is Mary who practices the art of holy hospitality by spending her time in the company of Jesus. Contemplation and solitude afford us the opportunity to quiet down, to settle down — to close our eyes as we open our hearts, so that when we open our eyes again, we see God playing with our children, or in the frantic cashier at the supermarket, or in the eyes of the stranger at our door.

Though Martha welcomes Jesus to her home, rather than focusing her attention on God, she is distracted by her many tasks. In her relentless busyness, she feels she is being used by her sister, imposed on by the company, working too hard while everyone else is hardly working. One can almost hear the ancient nursery rhyme that begins "Mary, Mary, quite contrary" playing in the mind as it applies to Mary's sister:

Martha, Martha quite contrary,
are you in the kitchen still —
with cupboards slamming and pots a'banging,
and an angry look that could kill.

When we read this story in the context of Luke's Gospel by remembering how it follows the parable of the Good Samaritan, we begin to sense the connection between contemplation and compassion. Recall that Luke shares these stories in the setting of the lawyer's question: "What must I do to inherit everlasting life?" We remember the answer to that question is simply, "Love God, love neighbor." In response to the lawyer's further interrogation about "who is my neighbor?" Jesus tells the story of the outcast, the Samaritan, to indicate that true discipleship is about living with compassion towards one's neighbors. We could also say that Jesus has identified himself with the one who is mugged, beaten and left for dead at the side of the road. Because Jesus has his eyes fixed on his destiny in Jerusalem, in the depths of his heart he knows this will be his fate. He will be stripped and beaten and taken outside the holy city to die. Sitting in Martha's house that day, reflecting on the story he has just told to the lawyer, perhaps Jesus is wondering who will stop and dress his wounds.

This becomes the better part: to focus our attention on the one who is about to die. Mary is in solidarity with Jesus and with all those with whom God stands in solidarity throughout all ages. Mary becomes a companion of Jesus on his way to the cross.

When we think of the Good Samaritan's compassion, an activist kind of love that sees someone in need and responds with care, we may connect him with Martha who is an activist as she tends to the needs of Jesus. But if the Good Samaritan story reflects one branch of the great commandment, "Love your neighbor," it is not Martha but Mary who gives witness to the other branch from which love of neighbor grows — namely, "Love your God." Mary sits at the feet of Jesus and listens to what he says. She hangs on every word that comes from the mouth of Jesus as if her life depends on it.

The attitude of compassionate discipleship praised by Jesus is one of paying attention. Compassionate action flows from the deep reservoir of communion with God found in contemplative prayer. True activism springs from still waters; from soaking in and being saturated with the Divine Presence.

Paying Attention

As I reflect on this connection between contemplation and compassion, I am reminded of a priest in my community, Father Rich Kolega. Just forty-eight years old, he was told by doctors that he had just six months to live. Shortly thereafter he came to live — and to die — at the place where I was living at the time. Though I was on the road much of the time Rich lived with us, whenever I was around him, I found myself being very much like Martha. I would ask him if he needed anything. I would try to address his present needs and wait on him in any way I could. I was trying to be hospitable. But perhaps I was also trying to avoid what I suspect Rich needed most: someone to sit with him, focus all one's attention on him, listen to his words, his stories, his soul.

After all, I like to keep busy, maybe because work covers a multitude of wounds.

But there was one day with Rich when the connection between contemplation and compassion became very clear to me. On December 8, the feast of the Immaculate Conception, a few of us celebrated Eucharist with Rich in our living room. That morning we found ourselves listening to Rich's words as he reflected on the Gospel story. He was struggling to say yes to his diagnosis, to the reality of his own death. He was trying to put his mouth around that reality. We sat at Rich's feet and listened to his words. It was a moment of standing close to someone on his way to Jerusalem and not being distracted by all the other appointments we had to keep, all the work we had to get finished, all the deadlines we had to meet. For this was a lifeline to understanding the meaning of discipleship. This was to choose the better part. This was to do what Mary did rather than being distracted by the many tasks we had to accomplish.

Without realizing it, we were practicing the prayer of contemplation with Rich that day — learning an important lesson about compassionate presence. Contemplation has been described as taking "a long, loving look at the real," and that is what we were doing: We were taking a long, loving look at the reality of life and death and God. We were focusing all our attention on the one who was about to die. We were emptying ourselves of all other distractions and seeing the real presence of God sitting in our living room.

That is what Mary was doing that day when Jesus came to Martha's house. Ultimately, balancing contemplation and compassion recognizes the value and importance of relationships: our relationship with God, with those we love, and with ourselves. When we spend time taking a long, loving look at the real presence of God in the world that surrounds us, in the prayers of our hearts that uphold us, in the eyes of each other that welcome us, we realize that we have chosen "the better part."

Living on Memory and Hope

Compassion lures us into the desert of solitude where the air is dry and hot. There she teaches us how troublesome and terrifying it is to be trapped in such an awful reality as human suffering. Solitude is not just the oasis in the wilderness where one can come and rest awhile — the place where one's thirst is quenched, one's hunger filled. No, solitude is more often the desert where dreams die hard and despair is easy. It is the wasteland where one lives on memory and hope.

In our solitude, memories crowd our souls. One summer I coached a little league baseball team for the YMCA. Most of my players lived in an inner city housing project. We practiced on Saturday mornings at a baseball diamond on a forsaken corner of what sociologists would call the "slums." But we were always the visiting team because the home team at this field really did call it home — at least to the extent that we call home the place where we sleep each night.

Every Saturday morning we found over a dozen nameless men with ancient eyes whose visions had been dimmed by the bottles of White Port they consumed each night before falling asleep at this field. I often wondered what story they had to tell and how they had come to sleep, perhaps even die, at this field of little boys' dreams.

Their shoes didn't match; their clothes were torn; their faces were filthy from the pillows of dirt on which they slept. Their bodies were fragile, unable to be nourished by cheap wine. These were men who heard the echoes of a time not worthy of remembering.

One old gentleman (at least he appeared gentle with the kind of face one might find on an overprotective grandfather) always watched the kids play. Infield practice served as his alarm clock. He seemed older than the others though it was difficult to guess his age. The warm breezes and cold winds that were his blanket made him seem older than he probably was.

Another man who was sleeping in center field one morning was awakened by a fly ball that dropped too close to his bed. He staggered a bit and shook his head to ward off the evil spirits that danced in his mind. As I followed his steps toward the gate, I noticed that he wasn't old at all. In fact, he was rather young — about my age. Perhaps he could have been my classmate. That cold reality made the scene more difficult to bear.

When practice was over, the boys left, but the old men stayed behind. One by one, they would leave the field for awhile. But they would not wander far because their lives were lived in a bottle. Like replicas of ships placed on the shelf, these men were remnants of a dark side of life most of us fail to see.

If the little leaguers were the stuff of which dreams are made, these men were the stuff of nightmares. Their field of dreams had become a field of despair.

When we seek a solitary space, memories like these will creep into our minds. At first we might look at them as distractions that must be driven away by a more persistent prayer. But in reality, far from being a detour away from the center of our soul, these memories are crawling out from our core to keep us on a compassionate course. We cannot understand the spirituality of compassion and the conspiracy it seeks to create until we take a trip to the dark side of life and seek to understand the suffering, the brokenness, the pain of those men on that baseball field. In them I saw the fragile nature of our humanity.

The hope in this journey to solitude is found in how Jesus went to the absolute limits of our emptiness, our aloneness, our alienation, to bring us back to communion with God. Jesus is the Word with the energy and power to transform the world by healing broken lives. But before the Word was given voice in the actions of his life, Jesus first spent time in his own wilderness. He went to the desert to be silent, to listen, and to feel the need of God.

In our aloneness with God in solitude and in the vision of a community that is characterized by this intimacy with our creator as we reclaim our heritage as "the beloved of God," we recognize the value of relationship, of seeing God visible and present in the other. But this recognition will allow joy to erupt and cascade like a fountain of mercy in the lives of those we touch only in the degree to which we have taken the time to drink deeply from the well of our own wounds and experienced the healing waters of God's care.

In the wilderness of compassion, we learn the importance of memory. We remember the great and gracious love of our God in sending the Son into the desert. Jesus desired to enter fully the human experience and so nothing we or our brothers or sisters in this world experience is foreign to God. I used to tell the students I taught at the Catholic high school in Sedalia, Missouri that indifference is the greatest sin. They got tired of hearing it, but I am convinced that not to care about the pain or loss or suffering of another, not to reach out in love to someone who needs us, not to allow the faces of the victims of our world's injustices, oppression, violence, famine and war to impact our lives — means we are not allowing the paschal mystery to become real and life-giving in our day. And unless the paschal mystery becomes real to us, we cannot become the real presence of compassion for others.

I think about those men sleeping in that vacant field, tasting the dirt of their terrible wilderness each night; I think of all those people who have died alone because there was no one there to care for them; I think of the many times I have yielded to temptations for power, for fame, for success and turned my back on the cross, and I know how difficult it is to follow Jesus into the wilderness of compassion and learn from him. But when we allow the look of those who are alone not by choice but by circumstance to break through our numb exterior and to settle in our souls, the hot, dry air of the desert begins to stir.

Praying Attention

When we enter the wilderness of solitude, we may come with many distractions and many expectations. But only one thing is needed; only one expectation can be met: to discover our true selves. Contemplation meets this expectation by inviting us to *pray* attention. In our prayer, we are attentive only to God. In one form of meditation, for example, we breathe in and breathe out, praying attention only to our breathing, to God breathing in us. In such a breathing exercise we become more centered. A gentleness embraces us. At the heart of this gentle Spirit is our true self. This gentle Spirit shapes us into a compassionate presence.

The practice of contemplation that leads to a life of compassion is captured in that old song which begins, "Getting to know you, getting to know all about you." When we get to know all about ourselves, when we unlearn some of the untruths that have shaped our lives and get beneath the labels that have defined us and confined us, when we come to the knowledge that we are holy, sons and daughters of the Most High, we are awakened to our true identity. By praying attention to God within us and by acknowledging our true identity as children of God, we are better able to pay attention to God within the other, thus becoming more fully human and more truly compassionate.

Exhaling the Breath of the Beloved

Called to be
Inclusive Co-Conspirators

After spending forty days and nights in the wilderness, the hot, dry desert air drove Jesus from solitude in search of community. In his solitude, Jesus had practiced breathing in the Spirit of God and now he was ready to exhale.

In the desert he learned what it means to be poor. Not so much a material poverty, but the quality he would later describe in his hillside homily as "poor in spirit." This spiritual poverty is the stance of being openhanded and openhearted. His time in the desert underscored his ultimate need for God as he relied on the weapon of God's Word to overcome the evil impulses that tempted him and threatened him to change his course. His sojourn into solitude not only deepened his identity as God's beloved but kindled his desire to be engaged in the work of God: the ministry of compassion. Now he was ready to enlist the services of some co-conspirators in this enterprise of bringing the reign of God's compassion upon the earth.

The first thing one notices in the call of the first disciples in Matthew's Gospel is how quickly the two brothers Peter and Andrew responded to Jesus' invitation to follow him. When Jesus called them out of their routine, they followed him *immediately* (Mt. 4: 20). There was no time to think, no time for Peter and Andrew to take care of their nets or the fish flopping around in the boat. Later, as Jesus saw two other brothers, James and John, fishing with their father, they also *immediately* "abandoned boat and father to follow him" (Mt. 4: 22). Discipleship required an immediate decision. There was no time for John and James to say farewell to their father or kiss their mother good-bye.

These first followers of Jesus took nothing with them except what they were wearing. They left the life behind they had known and risked losing everything, even their lives. Though they had no idea what would be in store for them, the miracles and misunderstandings, they threw caution to the wind and they did it for no other reason than that they were called by Jesus.

The story suggests that we need someone in our lives who will ignite the fire of desire in us, someone who will tap the great potential we have stored inside. This is what Jesus seeks to do for us. I don't know if those first disciples were looking for someone to inspire them, to motivate them, to give them the spark that would change their lives forever. But that's what happened. Because they were known by God they could risk everything and follow the way of compassion.

Still, the quick decision those first disciples made to leave behind their families and livelihood to follow an itinerant preacher might surprise us. After all, when we are faced with an important decision that will have lasting consequences for ourselves and our families, we are normally given some time to think and to pray about the decision. If the company you work for offers you a promotion, you would welcome the opportunity for advancement. But if this promotion meant relocating to another city, the decision about moving the family from familiar surroundings would require some time for all members of the family to talk about what such a move might mean. Perhaps the family might even visit the new city, tour some of the neighborhoods and check out the school where the children would be enrolled. This process of discernment is a healthy way for a family or an individual considering a change of careers to make a good decision about the future.

That is why the decision of the disciples to follow Jesus immediately seems almost unimaginable. Perhaps a better example for our culture of someone in Scripture who illustrates how difficult it is to respond to this call to follow the way of compassion is the prophet Jonah. He was called by God from his safe and secure environment to preach repentance to the Ninevites. Recall the story about how he was reluctant to go, how he took the long way around to get to Nineveh by booking reservations in a whale and how the whale spat him out on the shore of that great and decadent city.

Unlike the disciples who followed immediately, Jonah resisted God's call. And do you know why? Not because he thought he might fail, but because he might succeed! You see, the Ninevites were the enemy. Jonah wanted God to punish and destroy them. He prayed for their annihilation. Jonah refused to go to Nineveh at first because he was afraid that they might listen to his message and repent, and that God would forgive them!

Forgiveness was the last thing Jonah wanted for them. He did not want to offer the people the chance to repent. It's amazing, because all the other prophets we hear about in the Hebrew Scriptures suffer because their message was rejected. But Jonah suffers because his message was heard! And, sure enough, it only took the Ninevites one day to repent.

Lessons Along the Way

So what does all this have to say to us modern-day disciples? First, it suggests that we pause and reflect on those people in our lives who inspire us and motivate us and call forth from us our greatest potential. It may have been a parent, a grandparent, a teacher, a friend, a child, a co-worker, a boss or even a book that challenged us to dig deep inside and see the storehouse full of energy and excitement, vision and values we too often keep hidden and locked away. We have all known people like this who challenge us to expand our hearts and minds. In the space of our solitude, we reverence their memory.

Second, our conspiracy calls us to embrace the larger vision of who we are. By virtue of that Spirit of Jesus stirring in our souls, we seek to unleash our unlimited potential to love and forgive, to inspire and animate others. We are called to take the risks and dare the dreams and to do so for no other reason than because it is the Spirit of Jesus who motivates us to do so. Being the beloved of God means more than being passive recipients of God's grace. It means acting on, living out, our identity and becoming the beloved of others.

Third, it is important to realize that our fear at unleashing this unlimited potential of God's love in us is not always because we are afraid of failing. Sometimes, it is because we are afraid of success. Think about it. If we are successful, we will have to change the way we live and think and relate to others. For example, let's say there is someone I have been at odds with for years. All attempts to reconcile our differences have only increased the distance between us. I am resigned to the fact that this person will always be if not an enemy then at least someone I will never call a friend. And I can live with that.

Or can I? Am I afraid to try to reconcile with this person because I am afraid I will be rejected again? Or perhaps if I am accepted and welcomed as a friend, I will have to let go of all that stuff I loved to hate about this person for so long. I will have to treat, talk to, relate with this person differently — not with indifference or as an enemy but as a friend.

In effect, I have to become a new person, and the thought of letting go of "comfortable" or cherished ways of being may seem frightening. I am reminded that when the Berlin Wall came tumbling down in November, 1989, and the cold war began to thaw, there were some who voiced caution about the sudden flurry of freedom and friendship. They pointed out that the kind of reasoning that keeps people apart, separated into clearly defined groups of "friends" and "enemies" has a strong hold on our emotions. Many of us believe that there is no "us" without a "them." We need the bad guys, the people who embody all that stuff we want to get rid of — our greed, our anger, our sin.

Though the newborn disciples did not realize it that day on the beach, what Jesus was calling them to was a new way of thinking, a new way of living, a new way of loving. Following the way of compassion as lived by Jesus required that they become new people, not just variations of their old selves, but entirely new. This meant a new lifestyle, a new way of looking at old problems and failed relationships, a new way of seeing those they had been taught not to trust or had learned not to include in their company. As Jesus would show in his answer to the lawyer's question about "who is my neighbor?" Jesus was inviting the disciples to move to a brand new neighborhood where the welcome sign meant that all were welcome. These disciples were being invited to establish a new city, the city of God, where there were no city limits, no boundaries.

A New Spirit of Poverty

The lifestyle changes necessary to establish this new city of God with no limits were outlined by Jesus when he sent his disciples out on mission for the first time. After spending time in his company, watching his every move, listening to his every word, the students were ready to live what they had learned from their mentor. But before Jesus sent them out to practice what he lived and preached, he wrote a sermon for them: "The reign of God is at hand!" (Mt. 10: 7).

In order to be credible messengers of the in-breaking of God's reign, the hands of those sent must be empty and their hearts open or else God's energy that will "heal the sick, raise the dead, cleanse lepers, cast out demons" will not flow through them. They are to be channels of God's grace to those they will encounter, and the signal must be clear. If they are overly concerned about too many "things" — wondering if they brought enough clean shirts; worrying whether the batteries in their tape recorders are fresh; anxious about whether their shoes match the suit they brought — there will be too much static on the line and God's message will become distorted. People will turn them off.

One of the primary gifts disciples receive from Jesus is the poverty of compassion. This is the gift they are to give to others. Only by experiencing their own need for God will they be able to show others their need for God. Only by opening themselves to their own need for healing will others sense in them a means for their own healing.

The message of Jesus as he sends his first disciples out on mission is simple and straightforward: to travel lightly. There is a message here that goes deeper than how many possessions we have; how many books are on the shelf; how many clothes are in the closet. When we reflect on what it means to be a compassionate companion of Jesus, we are confronted with the question of our own poverty. Not just the surplus of material goods — though this can be an outward manifestation of our unwillingness to be detached. More important is the poverty that is found in compassion.

In poverty, we feel needy. In poverty, we become dependent. In poverty, we can lose ourselves in God. And it is only by losing ourselves in God that we will be able to find each other. The poverty of compassion frees us from focusing only on our own needs and allows us to enter, without distractions, into the needs of others.

But who among us likes to feel needy? The truth is, we like to be needed. We like to know that others depend on us because our identity is often entangled with what we do. As much as we may want to take a little vacation, we are worried that others will not be able to get along without us. It is only when we realize that others can get along without us just fine that we learn true poverty. When we acknowledge that the world is in God's hands, not ours; when we recognize that it is God's work, not ours; when we affirm that it is God's reign and that we are only a small but a privileged part of God's unfolding plan of building this new and holy city that we understand the poverty of compassion.

The only way we can play that part well is with empty hands and open hearts. By allowing God to awaken again that little child within us who will teach us how to be needy, dependent and poor, we will come to know that our identity is not defined by the work we do but by the love God has for us.

Learning a New Dance

Our movement toward the kind of poverty compassion calls us to also includes letting go of all those preconceived notions, those learned behaviors, of who to trust and who not to trust. This is a lifestyle change that challenges some of our most basic attitudes. Jesus alludes to how difficult and dangerous this transformation can be when he warns the disciples that he is sending them out like "sheep in the midst of wolves." Therefore it is necessary to learn how to dance with wolves.

The film *Dances With Wolves* tells a story of how this transformation is possible and some of the consequences it entails. At the beginning of the film, Lt. John Dunbar, a Union soldier in the Civil War, is wounded. It appears that he will lose his leg. Rather than the immanent risk of losing a limb in surgery, he chooses to risk his life on a suicide mission against the Confederate army encamped nearby. His daring ride inspires his comrades to attack, and they achieve victory.

His motivation seems clear: He feels he has nothing to lose so he risks his life. Confronted with the choice of going through life with one leg or dying, he chooses death. And in his dance with death, John Dunbar discovers life. Because of his heroism, he is given any assignment he desires, and what he wants most of all is to see the frontier. The rest of the film documents his moving to a remote outpost alone, his awakening to the Native American Sioux culture, his immersion in that culture and his ultimate realization that he is no longer John Dunbar, a soldier in the army, but "Dances with Wolves," a member of the Sioux people.

The turning point for John Dunbar is a moment shortly after arriving at the frontier when he has the opportunity to kill a Sioux who has wandered onto his post. Rather than giving in to the impulse to shoot first and ask questions later, Dunbar seeks instead to talk. But the Sioux runs away in fear. Later, Dunbar finds a young woman of the Sioux who is trying to commit suicide because of her grief over the death of her husband. Dunbar saves her and takes her back to the Sioux camp. Following these initial encounters, there is the slow, arduous process of getting beyond the barriers of language and lifestyle, fear and suspicion, until at last John Dunbar and the Sioux people find their common identity.

This process takes time. When Dunbar meets with the Sioux holy man, Kicking Bird, for the first time, the young woman whom Dunbar rescued serves as the interpreter. As a young girl, she had been rescued by the Sioux after her family had been attacked and all her relatives killed by a rival nation of the Sioux. She has not spoken English for many years, saying at one point, "The language is dead inside of me." But gradually the words come alive for her again and she serves as a bridge between Dunbar and the Sioux.

Like the parables of Jesus, *Dances With Wolves* teaches an alternative way of living. The story says it is possible to make friends with those who are supposed to be the enemy. When we unlearn the ways of the world and live in the realm of the reign of God, we discover in our brothers and sisters what John Dunbar discovered about the Sioux: a people of honor, of humor, of dignity, of dreams; a people, he wrote in his journal, devoted to family and dedicated to each other; a people who respect the integrity of the individual and reverence nature and creation. This, in the words of Kicking Bird, is "the great trail of a good human being."

But this learning process of becoming a new person while trying to let go of the labels that still linger in the back of our minds takes time, maybe even a lifetime. This should not discourage our efforts, however. After all, we have some good models in those first disciples who were chosen by Jesus to help us understand how difficult and treacherous it is to stay on the course of compassion and follow the great trail of transformation. Perhaps there is no better model in the Gospels of one who stumbled along this obstacle course on the way of compassion than the first person Jesus called, Simon Peter.

Peter Leadfoot

Earlier I referred to the question of identity when Jesus asked the disciples, "Who do people say that I am?" It is Peter who came up with the correct response. Jesus praised him because no one had told him Jesus was the Messiah. Peter's proclamation of faith came straight from his heart. In this scene, Jesus was so impressed with Peter's insight that he gave Peter the keys to the holy city: "I will entrust to you the keys of the kingdom of heaven. Whatever you declare bound on earth shall be bound in heaven; whatever you declare loosed on earth shall be loosed in heaven" (Mt. 16: 19).

Once he received the keys to the kingdom, Peter was in the driver's seat. But it's safe to say Peter had a lead foot at times — as in the very next scene in Matthew's Gospel when Jesus told his disciples he had to go to Jerusalem and suffer and die. Peter stuck his lead foot in his mouth, saying that it couldn't be so. Jesus responded to this one to whom he has just handed the keys, "Get out of my sight, you Satan" (Mt. 16: 23). Or there's the scene at the Last Supper when Peter refused to have his lead foot washed. Then at the table he boasted that even though every one else would run away, he would drive full speed ahead — only to take an early exit when the road to Calvary got a little rough.

So Peter, with his new responsibility of holding the keys to the kingdom, crashed a few times. But he kept the keys. Jesus never grounded Peter. He never took away the keys.

And I have to ask, "Why?"

Well, maybe the answer is found in Jesus' simple phrase of praise: "Blessed are you, Simon, son of Jonah! For flesh and blood has not revealed this to you, but my Father in heaven" (Mt. 16: 17). God had revealed to Peter Jesus' true identity. And because of this remarkable revelation and Peter's openness to receiving it, no matter how fast he drove, how many crashes he had, how many detours he took, he held on to the keys. Through it all, Peter learned a little bit more about the identity of the one he was called to follow. Through all the mishaps, he came to a deeper understanding of what it means to be a humble servant of compassion.

Dialogue about Discipleship

Thinking about this and how no one told Peter that Jesus was the Messiah, I heard this dialogue taking place in my mind.

Jesus asks, "And you, who do you say that I am?"

And I say, "You are the Messiah, the Son of the Living God."

And he says, "Good answer. But exactly how did you know this?"

And I say, "Well, others have told me."

And he says, "You mean, this wasn't revealed to you by God?"

And I say, "Well, not really. You see, I grew up in a family that had a deep devotion to you. I had good sisters in grade school who told me a lot about you. In the high school seminary, your name was mentioned all the time. By college, I thought I knew who you were so well that I took your identity for granted."

And he says, "Well, what about now?"

And I say, "Well, I still believe you are the Messiah, the Son of the Living God. But you know what? I wish I could say that God had revealed this to me. It seems I had all the answers about who you are before I even allowed God to speak to me. I mean, when I think about it, you had all the opportunities in the world to tell Peter and the others who you were. All the time you spent with them. You could have told them right there on the beach that day when you called them to follow. But you didn't. You didn't reveal yourself to them. Oh, I guess they could have gotten the hint. I mean, it isn't every day that they meet someone who heals the sick and raises the dead. Certainly all the miracles would have given Peter and the gang a few clues about who you are.

"But you waited for God to reveal your true identity. You waited for God to speak to the depths of their hearts so that when you asked the question, the answer leapt from Peter's mouth."

And he says, "So what are you saying? Do you feel cheated that others told you about me before God had the chance to plant the answer in your heart."

And I say, "Maybe."

And he says, "Well, maybe there's still time."

And I say, "What do you mean."

And he says, "Well, for example, when a friend stabs you in the front...."

And I interrupt, "You mean, the back."

And he says, "No, I mean the front. Enemies come up behind and stab you in the back. Friends betray you to your face. Sometimes with a kiss. Trust me on this one, I know. But back to my point, when a friend betrays you, then who do you say that I am?"

And I say, "What do you mean?"

And he says, "Well, when you've been hurt like that, how do you respond?"

And I say, "Well, how do you think I respond? I get angry. I carry the hurt around for awhile. I nurse the wound."

And he says, "That's what I mean: When you've been betrayed or hurt, who do you say that I am."

And I say nothing.

And he says, "Or remember that time, I guess it's about ten years ago now, you were sitting on the couch in Linda and Ron's house?"

And I say, "The names ring a bell. They are the names of a young couple I used to know in a parish where I once served."

And he says, "You were sitting in their living room the evening their four-year old son Luke drowned in the swimming pool."

And I say, "Yes, I remember."

And he says, "Do you remember what they asked you?"

And I say, "They kept asking who left the gate open to the fence surrounding the pool."

And he says, "Linda kept asking why. Why was the gate left open? Why had she talked on the phone so long and not noticed that Luke had wandered out the back door of the house? Do you remember how you answered those questions?"

And I say nothing.

And he says, "That's right. You said nothing. There was nothing to say. You just sat there with them. But in your heart you were asking, 'Now, who do I say that he is?'"

And I, lost in a memory I hadn't thought about for a long time, remain silent.

And he says, "You see, I could have told Peter and the others who I am right from the start. Do you think they would have believed me? They had to spend time with me. They had to listen and watch. They had to let go of some of their preconceived ideas about what kind of Messiah they were expecting. They had to go back to the Scriptures and reflect on the stories that were told about my coming into the world.

But most of all, they had to be open to receive the revelation from God that I am the one."

And I say, "Well then, why haven't I received such a revelation?"

And he says, "Haven't you been listening?"

And I say, "You mean, when I'm hurt or betrayed and question the meaning of friendship; or when a terrible accident takes the life of a four-year-old boy and I sit there with his parents not knowing what to say, that these are times when God reveals to me who you are?"

And he says, "Only when your heart is broken open can the truth of my identity get inside. Only in the sheer experience of living can the truth be revealed. Only when you have every reason not to love again because you've been betrayed once too often but still take the risk to love can you know the truth of who I am. Only when there are no answers to the tragedies and terrors of life can you begin to see I am the only answer."

And I say, "So that's why you told Peter and the others not to tell anyone that you are the Messiah? Each person has to come to the truth on his or her own."

And he says, "Not exactly, but you're close. You see, the truth of who I am is being revealed all the time. What's needed is for people like yourself not to take life for granted, not to take each other for granted, not to take the world for granted. Think about that friend who betrayed you. If you allow the betrayal to build a wall around your heart, not even God can get inside. Or think about that couple who lost their son. You couldn't give them any answer that would satisfy their minds or mend their broken heart. There are no words that heal such a wound. Nothing you could say could make up for the loss they would always feel in their hearts. But just by being there, even as they asked why, even as you questioned in your own mind who I am, the truth is revealed. And this is the truth: I AM. I am there, always. Always."

In Service of the Truth

The main obstacle Peter encountered in following this course of compassion was accepting the fact that the Messiah, the One who called him on the beach that day, would have to suffer and die. Though God had revealed to him Jesus' true identity, it took a long time for Peter to embrace the reality of suffering as a necessary requirement for compassionate discipleship. Peter had to taste the dust in the very depths of his despair before he could savor the true flavor of God's friendship found in One who called him.

In all the experiences, all the relationships, all the wounds, all the misunderstandings, all the triumphs, all the tragedies that compose our lives, the identity of the Messiah remains a secret until God reveals the truth in the depths of our own experiences. If we are open to this truth, if our hearts have been broken open to receive it, the answer to the question, "Who do you say that I am?" becomes obvious. In all these experiences, these incidents of incarnation, we find the key to the truth. It is a truth that ultimately makes us humble.

In giving the keys of the kingdom to Peter, Jesus envisioned a new holy city, a new Jerusalem. In allowing Peter to keep those keys even in the mishaps and misunderstandings that plagued Peter, Jesus affirmed that true leadership in the new Jerusalem comes not from the top of the temple but from the trenches. It comes not from a position of "standing over" but "standing with." Compassionate disciples of Jesus are humble enough to admit their need for God, always open to being healed and thus always ready to be ministers of healing.

In our search for the meaning of compassion and how we might breathe together in this conspiracy, we run heart-first and headlong into the question Jesus posed to Peter: "Who do you say that I am?" The answer to that question is found in our humble service of the truth that the Messiah is alive among us: in broken hearts and broken bread, in hearts filled to the brim with wonder and chalices filled to the brim with wine, in hearts that remain open even when it seems reasonable to close them, in minds that stay open when reason tells us to shut them.

This is the great trail of transformation the disciples embarked upon when they met Jesus that day on the beach. In his invitation to us to follow this way of compassion, the breath of the beloved whispers, "Be not afraid, and do not limit my wide mercy with your narrow minds and hearts." Inspired and motivated by the memory of Jesus, who opened his arms on the cross, who brought peace by the blood of his cross, we are invited to take the risks to reclaim our identity as God's beloved and embark on a new way of living. We dare to be disciples who think and act in an entirely new way precisely because we have been called by God.

Breathing Lessons

The Practice
of Compassion

Inspired by the breath of the beloved, the first disciples of Jesus embarked on the trail of transformation, the way of compassion. But we soon discover how difficult this course of compassion became for them. We want to believe that the compassion of God, brought to human form in Jesus, is a natural instinct in each of us — as natural as breathing. But we begin to see that most of the time it takes practice.

This principle of compassion does often come naturally in times of crisis and disaster. In times of natural disasters and unnatural acts of terrorism, people come together to help those in need. Many forget their own present needs and reach out to those who are directly affected by a disaster, offering help, hope and hospitality. But after the crisis has passed and we go back to the routine of our lives, what happens to our compassion? Do we put it back in the closet and reserve it for the next natural or human disaster?

The practice of compassion demands our full attention. It requires continuing formation in the study of our own wounds. In order to read, understand and respond to the wounds of others, the practice of compassion commands our paying attention to the injuries inflicted and the damaged people we encounter in the daily routine of life.

One sunny Sunday morning shortly after I arrived in St. Joseph, Missouri to begin ministry as a deacon at St. Francis Xavier parish, the phone rang at the rectory. An old woman's voice spoke softly. "I'm hungry," she said. "Could you give me a loaf of bread, maybe some butter and milk — anything you can spare to help me until my check comes in."

I was in between Masses and was tempted to give her the number of Social Services or a local food pantry. But because I was so new, I didn't know what resources were available. So I told her I would stop at the grocery store after the last Mass that morning.

She lived in the back room of a dilapidated apartment house. Poverty was etched in the lines of her face; her frail frame and hollow eyes mirrored her hunger. She was grateful for the food I brought but she didn't say much. Both of us realized that the sack of groceries might last a few days, but her poverty would linger. She was another anonymous victim of hunger in a land of plenty.

I don't remember that woman's name or where she lived, but I will never forget the hungry look in her eyes. When I looked into her hollow eyes, her expression reminded me of a story I once heard about a naive young missionary on his first assignment in a Central American village. He introduced himself to a parishioner. Detecting a certain smugness, an air of superiority, in the young priest's offer of help, the woman said to him: "If you have come to help me, you are wasting your time. But if you have come because your liberation and salvation is bound up with mine, then let us work together."

This breathing lesson of how we share the same air space with all the hungry, broken, oppressed and forgotten people of our planet was missed by the disciples on that day they found themselves with Jesus in a deserted place where he had been teaching a large crowd (See Mt. 14: 13-21). Evidently the disciples had not yet learned to read this truth that is carried in the look of hungry people. When confronted with the sight of the tired and hungry crowd, they did not want to get involved. They wanted to let the people fend for themselves.

Most of us can identify with the disciples' response — or lack of response. After all, they were just being practical. The crowd was too large and their own resources were too small. Since most of us like to consider ourselves practical and sensible people, the disciples' desire to have Jesus disperse the crowd should not surprise us.

So can we imagine the look on the disciples' faces when Jesus had another idea. He saw the people's hungry look and it moved him to compassion. "There is no need for them to disperse. Give them something to eat yourselves." Picture the look of astonishment on Peter's face and imagine what he might have said. "Rabbi, open you eyes! Look at all these people! Where are we going to get enough food to feed them all? We barely have enough food for ourselves."

Well, Jesus had opened his eyes. He had seen the look of hunger. The disciples were sensible and practical, but they had not yet learned the look of hunger because they had enough food for themselves. They did not yet understand how their own liberation and salvation were intimately connected to all those hungry people in that out-of-the-way place.

Yes, the disciples were sensible and practical. But such sensibility and practicality have a shadow side that stifles creativity and suppresses the possibility of compassion. In the presence of Jesus, sensibility gives way to sensitivity. Jesus saw hungry people and wanted to feed them. He felt their need. How did Jesus develop such sensitivity? Simple arithmetic. The breathing lesson Jesus teaches the disciples in that out-of-the-way place is the arithmetic of compassion: Subtraction leads to multiplication.

The Arithmetic of Compassion

To practice this breathing lesson on how compassion adds up, remember the context for this miracle of the multiplication of the loaves. In Matthew's telling of this story, Jesus just learned that his cousin John has been killed by Herod. In order to save face in front of his guests at his birthday party, Herod had John beheaded when his wife's dancing daughter requested it.

Jesus' cousin John was dead. Someone Jesus loved had been subtracted from his life. Though John was killed by Herod to fulfill a foolish oath he had made in front of his guests, we know enough about the life of John the Baptist to realize he was really murdered for the truth he spoke, the truth he lived. When Jesus heard of John's death, he wanted to run away and hide. He wanted to subtract himself, withdraw, nurse his wounds, grieve. In the wake of the news of his cousin's death, Jesus wanted to retreat into solitude. He wanted to be alone with his thoughts.

And what thoughts must have crossed his mind! Thoughts of John and him growing up together. Thoughts of John's fiery temper fueled by his passion. The last of the fire and brimstone prophets, Jesus must have recalled John's austere, ascetical lifestyle — his stomach-churning diet of locusts and wild honey which caused a fire in his belly that burned brightly in his eyes. Yes, Jesus must have remembered that hungry look in John's eyes. John was hungry for the coming of God upon the earth. Maybe that's why Jesus could recognize the look on the faces of the hungry crowd that followed him that day.

Alone with his thoughts, Jesus must have recalled his encounter with John that day on the banks of the Jordan River after he had requested to be baptized. How surprised he must have been that John, a man of high drama and ecstatic soliloquies on center stage of the wilderness theater, wanted to retreat to the shadows, wanted to get out of the way. Decrease. Subtract himself while the new star took center stage.

But now John was dead. He had been killed for his strict adherence to the truth. He had learned the ultimate lesson of compassion: The truth will get you killed. His death formulated meaning in this equation of compassion. It is about subtraction. A subtraction of self yields a sacred sensitivity. Sensible people learn to shut up when confronted with the consequences for continuing to live the truth. But not John. And not Jesus.

So Jesus' desire for solitude, his desire to withdraw from the crowd to grieve his loss, confronted him with this awful truth: John's fate would be his too. This was his destiny. So it would make sense for Jesus to remain in solitude for awhile to reflect on what was ahead of him. Instead, his own pain at the loss of his cousin led him to a deeper sensitivity for the suffering of others. His subtraction led him to multiply the loaves to satisfy the hunger of those who followed him.

This breathing lesson suggests that compassion is not without risk. Jesus saw what happened to John for speaking and living the truth. What makes this miracle of the multiplication of the loaves so remarkable and risky is that John's death is such a fresh wound. Jesus could have chosen to follow the advice of the disciples and send the crowd away. He could have chosen not to get involved — at least not at this time when his loss is so raw and real. But when he looked into the faces of those people who had been following him and listening to his teaching, their faces became like a mirror reflecting back to him his own sense of loss, of grief, of hunger. He had to act, even if it didn't make sense, even if this desire to feed these people didn't add up in the minds of the disciples.

In the practice of compassion, this is an important breathing lesson. Jesus grieved the loss of his cousin John and sought at first some space and solitude to mourn his loss. But because his own heart was broken by the news of John's death, he couldn't keep the sufferings of others at arm's length. With heart broken open, he welcomed the vast crowd home to his heart. And he fed them.

The disciples, on the other hand, were like officials of the federal government wanting to wait for a real crisis before declaring this sight a disaster area and turning on their compassion. Jesus said to them, "This *is* a disaster area! Whenever there are people hurting and hungry, we can't wait for federal funds to trickle down. Give them something to eat yourselves."

Could it be that the disciples had not yet learned the arithmetic of compassion? Could it be they had not as yet suffered enough to be truly compassionate people? Could it be that their hearts had not been broken open enough for them to read the look in the eyes of others?

I am reminded of the story of the college student in his early twenties who was dying of cancer. One day he asked his teacher if he could see her about a paper that was due. But when he came to her office to talk about the paper, he said, "I can see in your eyes God has broken your heart too." He didn't know who or what had been subtracted from this woman's life that had caused her sorrow or pain. All he knew was that in the way she conducted her class, in the way she listened to her students, in the way she treated each one with reverence and respect, she knew her own suffering, her own pain, her own sense of loss and subtraction. He could read it in her eyes. It was the look in her eyes that quickened his hope that he had found a soul mate, a companion for his journey toward death. For the first time since his diagnosis, he felt he was not alone.

The multiplication of the loaves, the multiplication of compassion, can only be realized when suffering has subtracted so much of us that we have nothing left to give but what is left over. And it is in the leftovers — the baskets of bread that the disciples collected after everyone had had their fill — that we realize how compassion adds us. Those leftovers became the symbol of how Jesus planned to sustain the people after he had paid the ultimate price for his compassion.

The compassion and love shown by Christ that day on the hillside is evidence that the breath of God is always present in our hearts. All that is left for us is to allow that breath to flow through our actions to help others — not just in times of disaster, but in the most routine times as well.

Our liberation and salvation is bound up with those in our midst who are suffering, who feel separated, who hunger for food and thirst for justice. Our liberation begins when we recognize in the routine of our lives that there are people who live in poverty and pain every day of their lives. Our liberation begins when we allow their look to seep through the cracks of our own broken hearts and move us to compassion.

It all starts to add up: Subtraction of self, the subtraction caused by our own suffering, leads to the multiplication of bread. I saw this happen during my deacon year in St. Joseph, Missouri. The look on that hungry woman's face was the impetus for starting the House of Bread, a parish food pantry and financial assistance program at the parish. I saw the conspiracy of compassion evident in the people of the parish who got involved in reaching out to the poor and hungry of the city.

As Jesus looked at the faces of the hungry crowd on the hillside that day, he knew their pain. He saw it in their eyes. He realized that feeding them that evening would curb their hunger pangs for awhile but that there would always be more than enough hunger, suffering and pain. But he also showed that there would always be more than enough bread. The bread baked in the oven of one's own experience of loss. The bread of one's own tears, the bread of compassion.

A Star Student: Bartimaeus

Jesus tried to teach his disciples this first breathing lesson, the arithmetic of compassion, in the open air classroom of the hillside that day when he fed the multitude. But as we are aware from our reading of the Gospels, the disciples were slow learners when it came to the most basic breathing lesson taught by their teacher: The Messiah must suffer and die. Still, we are given numerous examples in the Gospels of people who were very advanced in understanding the course of compassion. One of these prize pupils is found in Mark's Gospel (Mk. 10: 46-52): the blind beggar Bartimaeus. In this story of the encounter between

Jesus and the blind son of Timaeus, we discover more breathing lessons.

Bartimaeus had spent his life in darkness, begging by the side of the road. But he did not give in to the temptation to give up. He did not give in to the temptation to be satisfied with the darkness. He did not give in to the temptation to cling to the way things were. Though he had been sitting by the road for a long time, he was aware that new life was possible. Bartimaeus had not lost the vision in his heart, even though he could not see the light of day. His conversion had already taken place; grace was already his, giving him the desire to cry out to Jesus, "Son of David, have mercy on me!" (Mk. 10: 47).

In the darkness of his life, Bartimaeus learned the breathing lesson of patience. But patience is not to be confused with passivity. The common advice given to someone who is suffering an illness, or grieving the loss of a loved one or going through a difficult time is, "Be patient." This counsel tells the person that if he or she just waits long enough, the trouble will go away and better days will come.

The quality of patience we are talking about here is similar to what Paul described in his letter to the Romans:

> We rejoice in our sufferings, knowing that suffering produces character, and character produces hope, and hope does not disappoint us, because God's love has been poured into our hearts through the Holy Spirit which has been given to us. (Rom. 5: 3-5).

Being able to breathe in so much patience that one is able to exhale the fresh air of character, hope and love is difficult to practice. This is especially true in our age of drive-through windows at fast food chains and banks, pictures developed in an hour and places where we can get our oil changed in ten minutes.

Patience is the blossom of solitude. It flowers in the silence, almost unnoticeable until suddenly it erupts in full bloom. But the blossom often has a short life span and soon withers from neglect. One needs a stretch of silent space each day to nurture the flower's growth. In the rich soil of solitude, the buds of patience grow, silently, waiting for their moment to be born.

Cultivating the quality of patience allows us to hold even the most difficult people and situations in our hearts. For when we hold them in prayer, we are placing their names before God. We are allowing God to handle them! And God does handle them — with care. Patient prayer is the holy ground from which our dreams for a just world begin to grow. Just as farmers must have patience and trust that the seeds they plant in spring will yield them an autumn harvest, so patience is our guide. I am reminded what a very good and wise friend once told me. When confronted with one of my bouts of impatience, she said, "You can't hurry God. God will take care of things in God's own time. And God's always on time."

Her words struck me because I knew they were born from her own experiences of waiting. She had carried the weight of more than thirty years as a rectory housekeeper. She started working at the rectory when she was young because her family was poor. By the time I met her, she no longer needed the money (not that working for the church had made her rich), but she enjoyed being involved in the lives of the priests and people of the parish. At least, most of the time she enjoyed such involvement. For I knew that tears had washed her pillow every now and then over the years. She shouldered the disappointments with a smile and shrug. Her faith in a just God was deep. Her hope in God was strong. Her love for others was contagious. And she really lived the belief that God is always on time.

We reflect such patience when we listen to God's unspoken word in the silence of our hearts. Here in the silent space of our prayer we not only deepen our desire for God but increase our capacity for understanding our own experiences of suffering — those times in our lives when our bodies have been stretched out on the cross and our flesh nailed to the wood. Like Jesus, with arms outstretched to embrace the cares and concerns of all the world, the breath of God stretches our hearts in compassion and we find the courage to raise our voice and come out of the crowd knowing that God's time is our time. And our time is God's.

Bartimaeus had practiced such patience all those years he begged by the side of the road. But when he heard the excitement buzzing around him that the rabbi was nearing the place where he sat and waited, he realized his time had come.

Most people probably thought nothing about this blind man sitting by the side of the road. He had become a part of the landscape. They had become accustomed to his scent, his odor of decay. But then Bartimaeus raised his voice. He took the risk to scream above the din of the crowd.

The irony is that until he raised his voice, the people probably did not *see* him. He went unnoticed until he shouted out the secret: "Jesus, son of David!" They scolded him at first, "Shut up! Don't bother the Master! He's too busy for some blind beggar like you!" But Bartimaeus would not heed their advice. He dared to let go and with great passion shouted all the louder: "Son of David, have mercy on me!" (Mk. 10: 48). We sense how his years of patient waiting did not give Bartimaeus a passive spirit but an active voice. His patience in waiting for God's time to become his time had given him a voice of compassion (*with passion*). Even though he could not see Jesus with his eyes, he had seen him with the vision in his heart, recognizing him as the Messiah. This vision, learned through the years of sitting by the side of the road, gave him his voice.

Jesus heard this voice of Bartimaeus above the din of the crowd that was pushing in around him as he walked along the road in the same way as he saw the look on the faces of the hungry crowd. In the context of Mark's Gospel, this encounter with Bartimaeus occurs immediately after he has reminded the disciples again that he must suffer and die. Zebedee's sons, James and John, have just approached him with the request to give them seats near him when he entered into glory. Jesus asked them, "Can you drink the cup I shall drink or be baptized in the same bath of pain as I?" (Mk. 10: 38). Zebedee's boys said they could, and Jesus promised that they would drink from this cup of suffering and be baptized in this bath of pain. But it is clear from the discussion that followed that the disciples did not understand the implications of drinking this cup or taking this bath. Instead, we learn that the request of James and John caused dissension in the classroom among the other student-disciples. They resented Zebedee's sons requesting such high places at the awards banquet at the end of the term. Jesus must have sighed at how slow these chosen students were, for they still missed the point of his breathing lessons. "It cannot be that way with you," Jesus said to his students. "Anyone among you who aspires to greatness must serve the rest" (Mk. 10: 43).

In teaching the disciples this important lesson about true leadership, Jesus touched again the truth that he would suffer and die. He would drink fully the cup of suffering and be immersed in the bath of excruciating pain. Because he was in touch with this truth, being sensitive to the cries of the poor came spontaneously. His hearing was acutely attuned to the sighs and screams of those who needed him. This is why he could pick out the voice of Bartimaeus from the crowd. And so the stage was set for the meeting between the teacher and the gifted student.

Bartimaeus' prayer, "Son of David, have pity on me," was answered as Jesus stopped and said, "Call him over." When Jesus issued this invitation, the people changed their perception of this nobody beggar and helped him to his feet.

Unlike the disciples in the preceding story, who immediately after learning they would have to drink from the cup of suffering and be immersed in a bath of pain got into an argument about who among them was the greatest (an argument which was to surface again at the Last Supper), Bartimaeus was ready to respond to Jesus' invitation because he had spent his life drinking from the cup. He had spent his life getting drenched by the rain of pain as he sat by the side of the road. Because Bartimaeus had been part of the depths of life and knew what it feels like to be ignored, stepped on and spat upon; because the soil of his heart was rich with suffering, invitation and response could blossom.

This breathing lesson emphasizes that God is the one who calls, but it is the disciple's responsibility to call out to God in prayer as Bartimaeus called out to Jesus. We learn this lesson when we keep hope alive even as we taste the sorrow in the cup of suffering, even as we are soaked to the bone in the bath of pain. Bartimaeus listened to this hope beating within his heart. In listening to this voice of hope within, he learned that God is always there inviting us to a deeper union. By first listening to the God he discovered in his pain, Bartimaeus found his own voice.

God's invitation to hope is captured in the covenant God made with our ancestors in faith. This covenant is described by the prophet Jeremiah: "I will put my law within them, and I will write it upon their hearts; and I will be their God, and they shall be my people" (Jer. 31: 33). The prophet gives the people a symbol of promise and fidelity even in the midst of their darkest hour of exile. The covenant between God and the people, once written on stone and so easily chipped and shattered and broken to bits, is now written upon their hearts. Jeremiah challenges the people to allow God to sign God's name on their lives: "You are mine." These words of love are not spoken but are written with the pen of compassion.

As we know, spoken words tend to sink in for a time but after awhile become fleeting memories. "What exactly did she say? It was so poetic, I wish I would have written it down." On the other hand, words of love written on paper last a lifetime. We can take a letter out of the drawer and read the words again and again and be reminded that we are loved — until, finally, they become etched upon our hearts. And words of love written on the heart last an eternity.

Bartimaeus had internalized the covenant, the relationship that reinforced his identity as one of God's special people (even though his blindness might have offered evidence to the contrary). In the sanctuary of his heart, he had come to believe that God's grace was with him, consoling him, inspiring him and energizing him, even as he walked in the dark.

The Practice of Prayer

In the exchange that followed between Jesus and Bartimaeus, we learn how this lesson of breathing in (listening) and breathing out (speaking) leads to discovering how our attitudes about prayer influence our understanding about compassion. Jesus asked Bartimaeus what he could do for him, and the blind beggar responded with the prayer of compassionate discipleship: "Master, I want to see" (Mk. 10: 51).

These words of Bartimaeus become our morning prayer, our dream at dawn. It is the prayer on the lips of every companion of Jesus who desires compassion. It is the only prayer one needs to utter in the presence of the Holy One: "God, let me see." Indeed, Bartimaeus already was able to see more clearly than most of those surrounding Jesus that day. His inner eye had been open for some time, waiting patiently for the opportunity for God's shadow to pass over him.

This simple prayer, "God, I want to see," is challenging because it forces me to ask, do I really want to see? For such seeing ultimately leads to following Jesus to that destination where I am invited to drink from the cup of suffering and be immersed in the bath of pain. Certainly it would be much safer just to sit by the side of the road and make up stories of a savior rather than raising my voice with the request, "I want to see." But prayer is pivotal if we are to come to know and understand the suffering of Jesus, as well as our own pain and the suffering of others. Prayer is our teacher, and the breathing lesson is how to become like our prayer.

One woman I've met along the way who practiced this quality of prayer was a simple, elderly woman named Nellie. She lived alone and was in the last stages of a long battle with cancer. The first time I visited at her tiny apartment to bring her communion and the sacrament of the sick, I noticed that most of her possessions were still in boxes since she had only recently moved in. She had come back to the city where she was born. She had come home to die.

One of the few things she had unpacked was a battered crucifix which hung on the wall across from her bed. The corpus was broken, held together with tape. One of the members of the parish staff had seen this crucifix on a prior visit and bought her a new crucifix, which he asked me to give to Nellie. As I hung it up for her to replace the older one that had become battered with age, Nellie told me that at night when she lay in bed the cars coming down the street would spotlight the crucifix. The broken body of Jesus would be illuminated by the cars' headlights. It gave her a prayerful reminder that she wasn't alone in her suffering. Jesus was there. With that assurance, she could fall asleep each evening.

In those last days of her life, Nellie had become her prayer.

Real prayer is not the multiplication of words but the subtraction of self. Nellie taught me that so much of what I pass off as prayer is merely words — pious ramblings and chants and rants and raves designed to get God's attention. She was a living example of what Jesus taught his disciples about prayer. He told them "When you pray...go to your room and shut the door and pray to your Father in secret; and your Father who sees in secret will reward you" (Mt. 6: 5-6).

Prayer is an attitude of allowing God to increase in us as our urgings of ego decrease. It is not a matter of fulfilling our wants but of satisfying our need for God; of deepening our desire for God. This quality of prayer, practiced by Bartimaeus as he sat in the dark by the side of the road and by Nellie as she gazed upon the broken body of Jesus on the cross, opens our eyes to the presence of God's covenant, even in our pain. It opens our ears to listen to God in silence as we strain to hear again the great power and promise of prayer: "Ask, and it will be given you; seek, and you will find; knock, and it will be opened to you" (Mt. 7: 7).

Our prayer need not be filled with a lot of words as if our words piled on top of one another might by chance reach heaven. A good example of this proper disposition for prayer is found in the familiar story from Luke's Gospel about the Pharisee and the publican, or tax collector. If Bartimaeus' prayer, "God, I want to see" is our morning prayer, then the tax collector gives us our evening prayer: "God, have mercy on me, a sinner." This is the whisper of the lowly one that punctures the heavens and reaches the ear of God. It is the prayer of one who seeks to serve God in all things, knowing that at times she stumbles and falls, but confident that her prayer finds a home. It is the prayer of one who humbly admits his need for God.

We are probably not surprised that God hears the prayer of the publican even though we may forget that this man was a traitor in the eyes of his people. As a tax collector, he sold out his own by working for the oppressors. Yet he came to God seeking only pardon and peace. Standing in the back of the synagogue, he kept his head bowed low, not daring to lift his eyes toward heaven. He knew that his sin was always before him and so gave voice to the only prayer he could say: "God, have mercy on me, a sinner."

The publican's posture of prayer is contrasted sharply with that of the Pharisee, the holy one, who stood straight up and thanked God because he wasn't like everybody else. The Pharisee stood in the front of the synagogue so that everyone could see him. He looked down upon the tax collector and others he deemed sinners. This man was so full of himself that there was no room for God.

The hard part about the kind of prayer practiced by this publican, Bartimaeus and Nellie is how difficult it is to face the truth that sits in silence in the sanctuary of our souls. The truth is that we are not self-sufficient, that there are parts of our lives we need to work on, that we fail at times to follow in the footsteps of Jesus, that we hold on to hurts and nurse grudges too long. In the silence of our prayerful hearts, we stand empty and so are able to hear our God knocking at the door and longing to come inside. Too many words insulate us from our inner poverty. Too many words drown out the sound of God's voice at the door.

Shortly before I was ordained a deacon, the priest who was giving me my directed retreat gave me an insight that has helped me greatly in praying the Liturgy of the Hours. I had told him I was uncomfortable with the Divine Office as a format for prayer. He said to me, "Don't worry so much about 'getting the Office in.'" Instead, he advised me that if I was struck by a word, a phrase or a psalm, I should stay with it. "Don't hurry past it," he said. "It is God knocking at the door."

Prayer is a constant struggle, and perhaps I see so little change in myself and in my world as a result of my prayer because I don't allow God to change me. Perhaps I'm afraid of the silence in my own heart; afraid I will hear the knock on the door, afraid that my prayer indeed will change me, afraid to become my prayer.

But if we believe that it is the Spirit breathing within us, praying within us; if we are willing to practice each day by taking some time in the morning to echo the words of Bartimaeus, "God I want to see," and some time in the evening to make the prayer of the publican our own, "God, have mercy on me, a sinner," then we will touch the truth Nellie found as she looked upon that battered crucifix: We are not alone. When we know this truth that we don't have to go through the suffering and pain alone, we begin to gather the courage and resolve to follow the way of compassion.

The Practice of Faith

The prayer of Bartimaeus flowed from his faith — the graced awareness that had been growing within him. Because of his faith, Jesus brought the blind man the wholeness he desired: "Go your way; your faith has made you well" (Mk. 10: 52). Those words pack a punch! Both of those phrases point to a profound truth about the practice of compassion. First, because of his encounter with Jesus, Bartimaeus could not go his own way; rather, his way had become the way of Jesus. At the end of the passage we read, "And immediately he received his sight and followed him on the way." This breathing lesson reminds us that when one has encountered the Lord, one can no longer follow one's own path, pursuits or preconceived patterns of life. No, when one has been touched by the healing presence of God, a new road opens for us, a road mapped out by Jesus. It is a road marked by a conspicuous signpost: the cross. No longer could Bartimaeus sit still; he had to follow. The force of his faith fueled his tired, aching legs and put them in motion, and he followed Jesus on the way of the cross.

The second phrase of Jesus' life sentence, "Your faith has made you well," offers us an intriguing proposition. Those words occur often in the Gospels in the context of Jesus' healing ministry. What do they mean? What are the implications? The obvious answer seems to be that without faith, healing is not possible. Unless Bartimaeus and so many others in the Gospel cooperated with God's grace, Jesus would not have been able to give them the healing they desired.

Of course, the faith of Bartimaeus was a gift from God in the first place, so it is ultimately God's power that did the healing. But the gift had to be accepted, embraced and cultivated over the years of waiting. Bartimaeus' *yes* to God's gift actually completed the circle of healing. Without his *yes* to God, he would have remained sitting on the side of the road, telling others about all the commotion that day, but staying confined in darkness.

Instead of just making a legend of this carpenter of Nazareth, this holy one he named as Messiah and savior, Bartimaeus said *yes* to his inner call. As a result, he joined the life of the savior by following him up the road to the ultimate destination for all disciples: Calvary.

Faith is such a fragile gift. It is most graphically expressed and most severely tested in those moments of crisis when we run headfirst into the sign of the cross. Faith is so easy to take for granted until push comes to shove, until darkness eclipses light, until laughter gives way to tears, until sorrow and sadness stalk our every step. Sure, it is easy to believe when everything is right with our world, when the blessings seem abundant, when all the breaks go our way. But what becomes of our faith in times of trouble and turmoil, tension and tragedy? How deep is our faith when our dreams have turned to dust? How strong is our faith when our hope is shattered like a piece of glass on the sidewalk?

There's an important breathing lesson here about the connection between faith and prayer. Faith allows us to believe in God even when God seems to be absent. Faith allows us to pray even when God seems to have put us on hold. Why bother to blame God for God's inactivity in our lives if we didn't believe God exists? Why bother to shake an angry fist at God in the aftermath of tragedy if we didn't believe that God is still there, somewhere, somehow to be found amidst the ruins of our broken lives? Why bother to whisper, let alone scream, at God if we didn't know deep in our heart that God is still moving and breathing and living within us?

Our faith affords us the vision to see God's redemptive action at work even when obscured by the most tragic and terrifying moments of our lives. Even in the blood and tears of the cross. For our faith is based on a vision that will not disappoint; a vision that will be realized in God's own time, God's own space, God's own way.

Faith allows us to see the vision reborn in the gentle words of a friend who comes to share our grief. We see the vision awaken in the eyes of the grandmother who is visited by her granddaughter at a nursing home. We see the vision erupt in the tens of thousands of people marching in Washington to demand more money for the fight against AIDS or to remember friends who have died and now have their names and memories stitched upon a quilt. We see the vision enacted in those who give their time and energy and talent to build homes for the poor. We see the vision etched in the eyes of the dying one who is grateful for our visit, our touch, our prayer. We see the vision articulated when people speak with courage for Gospel values when they are compromised at the work place.

The prayer on the lips of the disciples, "Increase our faith!" (Lk.17: 5), becomes our prayer too. Our challenge as students seeking to learn the way of compassion by practicing the breathing lessons offered us by Jesus is to make that prayer come alive in our actions; to make it more real in our relationships with others; to make it stronger as we confront the death and destruction, the pain and sorrow, the wounds and war, the apathy and anguish that so often color our age.

Even the smallest, simplest act of faith may awaken in others the vision. It may move another to believe. It may help another to feel less alone. No, we may not be able to move the Rockies with our faith, but we may just be able to keep the dream, the vision, alive long enough for others to see and to experience the presence of God. And every gesture of faith we make strengthens our own connection to the vision of compassion. In sharing this vision of compassion, in breathing together for goodness' sake, we come to understand how subtraction caused by our own suffering leads to a multiplication of our love. Here we learn that the answer to our prayer is found in the love we share.

Breathing Together

Conspiring to
Create Community

The effect of practicing the breathing lessons outlined in the last chapter is to come to a deeper realization that we are known and loved by God. This knowledge leads us to embrace our identity as people capable of compassion. When we practice these breathing lessons, we begin to sense a desire to come together with others to share our experiences. By articulating our experiences, we deepen our understanding of what it means to be compassionate.

In the sharing of these stories of faith, we trace the threads in the tapestry of our own experience. These experiences are the pieces of cloth we have to work with in making the quilt of compassion that will warm our nights, our bodies and our souls. One of those pieces in my story occurred when I took a leave of absence from my studies for the priesthood. Taking time away from the religious community that had welcomed me, educated me and challenged me was one of the most important decisions of my life, for it gave me a me a deeper and wider understanding of community.

I lived in a one-room apartment of a boarding house in midtown Kansas City. There was a single light bulb dangling from the ceiling in the dreary hallway on the first floor. This was the light that lured Andy home. He stumbled a bit and begged the wall to support him as he fumbled for the key to his one-room apartment. He softly sang, "It's a long way to Tipperary," raising his voice only slightly when he was sure of the words. Dropping his key, he tried to pick it up, but instead followed it to the floor. There Andy slept until morning.

Once again the hall was Andy's bed for the night. But it didn't matter a great deal, for this old man lived most of his life within the four walls of his sparsely furnished cell. Though his name wasn't really Andy, Andy was real. His life was a dark mosaic of pool halls, dangerous alleys and damp flophouses in cities too numerous to count. Andy had seen them all and slept in most, and he relished the chance to tell his stories.

The summer I lived in the same building as Andy was unbearably hot — more than a month of 100-plus temperatures. That was the topic of one of our conversations as I was going to play tennis and he was coming back from lunch, the leftovers he didn't drink tucked under his arm.

"I don't know if I can take too much more of this heat," Andy said.

"Ah, it will break soon," I reassured him, more intent on playing tennis than being neighborly. Fortunately, Andy wasn't in the mood to talk either. He wanted to finish his lunch.

Andy was careful to camouflage his drinking, but the reddish hue that colored his face gave his secret away (even when he wasn't sleeping in the hall). Andy liked it at this apartment house. The rent was cheap. The Salvation Army Thrift Store was right around the corner. The remnants of a once-prosperous shopping district were nearby. And with four bars within a block, the location seemed like heaven to Andy.

The six months I spent living in that apartment building with Andy and an elderly couple you will meet in a moment were important not only because of the people, but because of the space. I took time away from a lifestyle (studying for the priesthood) that had become too comfortable. Seminary life was all that I had known since I was thirteen. During those six months, I was away from the people I had lived with for years. In that space and time, I listened and learned a great deal.

I became an expert on where the lines of cracked plaster led; on where the ceiling light used to be before it was painted over; on how many roaches to expect the day after the exterminator sprayed. I fell asleep to the endless drips from the leaky faucets and awoke to the drone of country music from the apartment next door.

Living there in that apartment building with Andy and the others — many whose faces I can't recall and whose names I never heard — was a step away, a step out of line, a step into a world that was at first strange and yet became more familiar than fascinating. Quiet and empty most of the time, the building was filled with the sounds that silence and the city conceive. Though Andy and the others have become a faded photograph in the album of my life, the impact of my time with them survives. The images of that place are strong in my soul. It was time well spent because I learned about the God of the street, listened to the silence and found a way to say yes to ordained ministry in the church. It was a yes that was intimately connected with Andy's life of quiet desperation.

Andy had been a part of the depths of life. He stood under the weight of bad breaks and bad luck and bad choices. And in standing under them, he came to understand that this is precisely the place where Jesus stood so often in the Gospels. For Jesus listened to the stories of people like Andy who had been pushed or shoved or sometimes even chose to live on the fringe of society. He stood in the place where they stood. Sometimes he shared a meal with them. Sometimes just a story. These people whom the world or the church or society had given up on found in Jesus a companion for their journey. It was a journey that led them from the fringe of doubt to the very center of a field called faith. It was a journey they walked with Jesus from the outskirts of the city to the hub of Jerusalem and then back again to a lonely hill outside the city where Jesus died with them. It was a journey to an unmarked grave from which they would rise again with him.

Andy's life showed me this mystical map through those mine fields where my next step could trigger an explosion of pain and sorrow. Andy had not given up on life because he knew God had not given up on him. Though he was not able to articulate it in the language of faith, in listening to his story I heard sacred sentences and prophetic phrases. In between the lines of Andy's stories, I read the handwriting of God which authored a single Word, Jesus, who defines the meaning of compassion.

Jesus, the Word made flesh, made himself at home on the fringes of life. Here, on the edges, he listened to the stories of people like Andy. In his listening, he moved the center of community to the edge. The people on the edge, on the fringe, became the center of his attention and affection. But Jesus did not only listen to their stories, he learned from them.

Listening and Learning

A good example of how Jesus conspired with people on the fringe and how he learned from them is the story of the Canaanite woman (Mt. 15: 21-28) who comes out of the crowd and starts shouting to Jesus using the Messianic title "Son of David." As we saw in the last chapter with Bartimaeus who also called Jesus by this title, our first impression of this woman is that she would be an unlikely source to recognize Jesus as the Messiah. But she does because, like Bartimaeus, she is part of the fringe community. She is one of the outsiders. This woman, who because of her ethnic origin is an outcast and because of her religious background is considered a stranger to the covenant, recognizes Jesus as the Messiah and asks him to heal her daughter.

At first Jesus ignores her. But as a mother concerned for her daughter who is being tormented by a demon, she won't give up easily. She wants to be noticed, so she continues to call out to Jesus.

Recall how the narrow-minded disciples urge Jesus to get rid of this pestering pedestrian from the other side of the religious tracks. Jesus, trying to keep an open mind, is gentle, perhaps even apologetic, in his rebuttal. "I was sent only to the lost sheep of the house of Israel" (Mt. 15: 24). Remember, Matthew's Gospel was written primarily for a Jewish-Christian audience, so these words regarding the narrow scope of Jesus' mission should not surprise us. What might surprise us, though, is this woman's response. She doesn't go away but instead comes even closer. She kneels before Jesus and prays, "Lord, help me." And what may surprise us even more is what appears to be the rudest remark on the rabbi's record. Jesus says, "It is not fair to take the children's food and throw it to the dogs." He calls this woman from Canaan a canine. And she doesn't seem to mind. Indeed, her dogged determination to help her daughter gives rise to one of the most remarkable faith responses in Scripture. "Yes, Lord, yet even dogs eat the crumbs that fall from their master's table" (Mt. 15: 27).

With these words, this woman from Canaan, this outsider, seems to open Jesus' mind to new possibilities and new parameters for his mission. Her faith astounds Jesus and he immediately heals her daughter. Now, we can argue that Jesus was just testing this woman's perseverance and her faith. Or we can say he was holding up this woman as an example to stretch the narrow minds of his disciples. But however we hear this story, the point is that in this encounter with the Canaanite woman, Jesus now sees that in God's house, in God's heart, there is room for everyone.

When we take this teaching to heart, its meaning begins to stretch our hearts' walls and strengthen our resolve to be an inclusive people of compassion. So, how inclusive are we? How much room is there for those in our lives whose views are different or even contradict our own? Though we may pride ourselves on having open minds and open hearts, remember that we can cram a lot of prejudice and intolerance into those open minds and hearts. As we seek ways to conspire with others for goodness' sake, we must take an honest look at how often we clutter our open minds and hearts with attitudes and views that exclude rather than include. And how often in the name of religion — and sometimes even in the name of God — we keep people out of our cozy and comfortable little circle of companionship.

I am reminded of the story about Mahatma Gandhi when he was a student in South Africa. He had become deeply interested in the Bible and was particularly impressed with the Sermon on the Mount. He gradually became convinced that Christianity was the answer to the caste system he had experienced in India. So he decided he would seriously explore Christianity and perhaps even become a Christian. One day he went to Church to attend Mass and inquire about instructions in the Catholic faith. But he was stopped at the entrance of the church and gently told that if he desired to attend Mass he was certainly welcome to — in a church reserved for blacks. Gandhi left and never returned.

This is a great challenge to our conspiracy. It is not only to find room in our hearts for a Gandhi, but also to find room for the one who turned him away at that church door. Gandhi, of course, like the Canaanite woman in the Gospels, took the rejection and allowed it to fuel his passion for peace among all races and religions. Like Gandhi, like that Canaanite woman, co-conspirators of compassion believe in creating community where all are welcome, where each one finds a home.

When Our Passion Gets in the Way

Many people are being excluded from an experience of community today on the basis of race, creed, gender, orientation, ethnicity. When people are excluded because of who they are or what they believe, the wounds inflicted tend to isolate and separate them from others.

The Canaanite woman teaches us how to overcome such isolation and separation. She is so persistent because of the love she feels for her daughter that she will cross any line, overcome any barrier, in order to have Jesus pay attention to her daughter's needs. It is her passion in finding a cure for her daughter and her creativity in responding to Jesus' exclusive remark that result in healing. And that passion and creativity flow from her faith.

We have already said how necessary finding one's passion is in developing a compassionate heart. But sometimes our passion can create obstacles rather than removing them. Sometimes we feel so strongly about a particular issue that we are blind to the positions held by those with whom we disagree. Sometimes we are so sure of the rightness of our cause that we exclude the views of others who might have something to teach us.

There is much talk these days about teaching tolerance to our children. Teaching tolerance is a good start, but I wonder if it is enough. After all, when I think of "tolerance," I think of "putting up with someone." The call to be compassionate that is shaped by a spirit of inclusivity means more than simply "putting up with our differences." It is more than just everyone "trying to get along." Rather than just "putting up with" or tolerating those with whom we disagree, our conspiracy invites us to see how honest dialogue can take us deeper into the mystery and the reality of God. We don't just tolerate another's way of seeing things; rather we seek to learn from others how their experiences can actually teach us something about God.

We can remain open and passionate, faithful and focused without having to close the door to another's point of view or religious tradition. This is what the Canaanite woman does. She remains open and passionate, faithful and focused, and in the process perhaps even opens Jesus to a brand new understanding of his mission.

As we seek to conspire with others for compassion, we might look at how passionate we are in living our own beliefs. Does our passion build obstacles, or does it create enough heat to burn away the barriers that keep people apart? What are those limits that keep us separate? So often what limits us are our fears of diversity. What limits us are our own insecurities. What limits us is our own inability at times to see the dignity and dreams of the other. What limits us is our failure to reverence the other's story that may help us to grasp why the person holds such views. What limits us is the prejudice we have crammed into our open minds.

When we reflect upon our passion, is our passion like that of the woman in the Gospel story — so focused, so forgiving, so faithful that it has the power to bring healing to others in our family, our community, our church, our world? That, it seems, is the measure of true passion: It doesn't divide; it brings healing.

Being compassionate seems to mean more than just tolerating our differences. It seems to point to something beyond welcoming those of various denominations or traditions and making them feel comfortable. It seems, instead, that being a compassionate, inclusive community implies a deep and abiding respect for the dignity and the dreams of those with whom we differ. It implies a reverence for the image of God that is carried in every human heart — a reverence that strives always to recognize the Divine Presence in each person and all of creation. Being inclusive doesn't mean denying our own beliefs or throwing water on our own passionate pursuit of God's presence. Being inclusive means allowing our core beliefs to expand our heart rather than close our minds; enlarge our vision rather than narrow our view; extend our compassion rather than limit our mercy.

Reverencing the Other's Story

The story of the Canaanite woman's faithful response to Jesus, a response that extended the boundaries of compassion, invites us to recall those times in our lives when our hearts were stretched by people we have met along the way. For me, Maude and Ben were two persons who did for me what the Canaanite woman did for Jesus.

I met them the summer when I lived in that single room boarding-house apartment. I didn't see Maude and Ben very much the first couple of months I lived there, but as the temperatures in July and August soared, I started to see them sitting on their back porch every afternoon when I got home from work.

Maude spoke with a lisp. She always wore the same colorful housecoat that looked as faded and worn as she did. Her bright green socks didn't quite cover her ankles. Her husband, Ben, didn't have any teeth left, which made his words a blend of wheezing and whistling. Ben also had arthritis, which was his excuse for doing very little — from rarely shaving to being unable to hold a job.

One afternoon Maude was in particularly good spirits because the Salvation Army had just brought them a fan. The relentless heat had turned their apartment into a pressure cooker, but instead of letting off steam, Maude let out humor. "At least the fan circulates the hot air," she said. "And old Ben certainly has a lot of that."

Talking with Maude and Ben that hot afternoon and many times after that, I began to put together the puzzle of their lives: how they arrived at this boarding house, with little money, little food and, I presumed at first, very little hope. But then Maude would smile and Ben would whistle, and I realized they had more hope than I could imagine. For just like Andy, what Maude and Ben most ached for was someone to share their story.

Before I met them, people like Maude and Ben and Andy were aliens to me. I always thought of them as imaginary characters dreamed up by a starving writer; or statistics in a government report calculating how many people lived below the poverty line. Here I was living in the same building as these "statistics," listening to their story. It was a story of moving from city to city — wherever Ben could find work. His health had never been good, so it was difficult for him to hold a job for very long. Now that he was crippled with arthritis, it was nearly impossible. They had to rely on whatever funds trickled down from the government.

Maude and Ben complained about the weather but never really about the way they lived. They were satisfied with the small meals they ate each day. "Heck," Ben would say, "some people ain't even got that." Though they never went to a church, Maude and Ben had great faith. "Oh, we don't have much, but what we got ain't bad," Maude once said. "Besides, God's looking after us. He has so far, and there ain't no reason I can see for him to stop now."

In the few short months I knew them, Maude and Ben taught me a lot about the kind of faith reflected in the story of the Canaanite woman. Their story was one of being pushed away and rejected, of bad breaks and hungry nights when there were not even table scraps to eat. But they kept their hope alive in a God who provides. Their attitude was reflected in how the poet-president of the Czech Republic, Vaclav Havel, describes hope: "...an orientation of the spirit, an orientation of the heart. It is not the conviction that something will turn out well, but the certainty that something makes sense, regardless of how it turns out." The difference between shallow optimism and enduring hope is that optimism says everything will turn out well; hope believes that however something turns out, it will all make sense if it comes from the wine cellar of God's heart and goes through the winepress of the wounds of Christ.

Andy, Maude and Ben had gone through the winepress. Their wounds were visible in their story. They taught me that community is defined not by place but by people; not by privilege but by the willingness to share another's pain through listening to another's story. People like Andy, Maude and Ben helped me to draw new boundaries of compassionate community. They turned my vision of what it means to be community with others upside down and inside out.

Moving the Margins

As we explore ways to breathe together, the manifesto for this conspiracy is found in all four of the Gospels, but especially in Mark's. As we have seen in the case of Bartimaeus, the Gospel of Mark shows how it is the outcasts who are the ones who really get the message of Jesus that he must suffer and die. It is the people pushed to the fringe, the rejected members of the establishment, who understand what Jesus means when he says, "Come, follow me."

Why did these people get the point when it took so long for Peter, James, John and the other insiders to make the connection? Perhaps it's because they knew what it means to suffer. They had grappled and grovelled in the gutter, and they knew deep in their hearts that the only way God could save them was to sit in the sewers of life with them. A God coming in triumphant glory and enormous power would be of little value to them. But a God who experienced the humiliation of being rejected, betrayed and crucified had the power to save them.

The outcasts understood this radical notion of power that marked Jesus' life. It was not the power associated with strength but the disarming power of forgiveness and love. It was the kind of power that would restore dignity. The compassionate companion of Jesus has his or her eyes focused on the reality of the cross. Like Bartimaeus who spent his life under the weight of the cross as he sat by the side of the road, the compassionate companion is called to embrace the cross and follow Jesus in the company of others whose dignity is restored by the inclusive love of God.

When one looks at the stories of Andy, Maude and Ben, and the stories of those with whom Jesus conspired in the Gospels, we are faced with the question of logistics. Just as breathing into our wounds in a way that invites God's presence involves creating inner space for even our most unwanted pain, breathing together in community means being inclusive of all; it means making room for all those on the fringes of society. The logistics of compassion are highlighted early in the Gospel of Mark in the story about Jesus being inside a house surrounded by a crowd while his family is standing outside begging him to come out so they could take him home (Mk. 3: 31-35). The story suggests that Jesus' immediate family is embarrassed by him. They think he has taken leave of his senses and probably want to take him home to get some rest. After all, look at the people with whom this aspiring rabbi, this student of Scripture, this hero of holiness, is associating: prostitutes and tax collectors, public sinners and people who betray their own country, blind people and beggars! Not the class of people with whom any self-respecting religious leader from the suburbs would want to be seen.

When he hears that his relatives are waiting for him outside, Jesus, pointing to the people sitting in the circle around him, says, "This is my family." The people on the fringe, the outcasts of society, the unwanted remnant of the community — these are the people Jesus stands with, sits with, eats and drinks with. These are the people he identifies as his community of believers. They are the ones who because of their suffering are more attuned to God's will and so form the inner circle in the company of Jesus. Simple logistics: The outsiders are on the inside; the insiders are left out.

The scandal of all this, the scandal of Jesus, still remains with us today. We look around and see the faces of the poor; we feel the hands of the homeless and hungry grasping for our attention; we hear the chains of those imprisoned in body and soul. These are members of our family, Jesus says. It is not that we forget our mother and father, our sisters and brothers who make up our immediate family. But now we must think in larger terms. Now we are united in Christ's blood, which makes all human beings part of the same family. Blood is the tie that binds; the force that allows us to stand up and defend any member of our family against unjust accusation.

But let's be honest: We usually ignore or are embarrassed by that aspect of the ministry of Jesus. We are ashamed of certain members of our family. At times our institutional church appears as the well-meaning if misguided family standing on the outside, saying, "Come out, Jesus, we want to take you home where you belong. We want to take you back to more comfortable, more appropriate, surroundings. The scandal has gone on long enough. Stop spending time with the divorced and the gays and all those people outside canon law." Conspiring together and creating communities of compassion require that we break down the walls of an "insiders only" church and welcome those we have pushed to the fringe. It demands that we open our eyes and see beyond the stain of sin to the heart of those who desire to do God's will but just can't quite pull it off. It demands that we listen to the deep sighs of those who have lost hope after running headfirst again and again into stone walls of condemnation. It demands that we cradle the cares of those oppressed and welcome back those who are alienated. It demands that we take the risks of rejection and resist excluding those deemed unacceptable until the walls come tumbling down.

The walls that now divide us have been built by human hands. Paul reminds us of this in the letter to the Ephesians:

> For he is our peace, who has made us both one, and has broken down the dividing wall of hostility, by abolishing in his flesh the law of commandments and ordinances, that he might create in himself one new (person) in place of the two, so making peace, and might reconcile us both to God in one body through the cross, thereby bringing the hostility to an end (Eph. 2: 14-16).

Claiming our identity as companions of Jesus compels us to recapture this explosive force of love that destroys the barriers we build between one another. This takes great courage because it means we must confront real issues, real people and real systems that seek to institutionalize poverty, hunger, homelessness, oppression and injustice. As Henri Nouwen has reminded us, true compassion leads to confrontation.

The force of our faith gives birth to this quality of compassion, because we believe in a God who suffers with us. We build this temple, open to all, on the foundation of Christ's love. The inclusive nature of Jesus becomes the cornerstone of this holy house. We are challenged today to become a "dwelling place of God" by allowing God's Spirit to make us inclusive.

We learn how to be that dwelling place from listening to the blind beggars like Bartimaeus and those we so easily categorize as the "dogs" of our society. We would do well to listen to those men and women who see Jesus for who he is: a human being/God with a mission of suffering, death and resurrection. Men and women who accept the mission unflinchingly and caress the cross with hope and love are the ones who will remind us of how far we have to go to enlarge the circle of our compassion. They are the ones with whom we are to stand in this conspiracy of love and service. They are the ones who help us reclaim the covenant God made with our ancestors in faith.

The Nature of Covenant

At the center of this conspiracy, this breathing together for goodness' sake, is the biblical notion of covenant. When we stand with those who find themselves standing outside the circle of community, we affirm our belief in the ancient covenant God made with our ancestors in faith that is signed, sealed and delivered in the new covenant of Christ's blood.

The nature of covenant, as I understand it from the Hebrew Scripture, implies trust. The Israelites were to have an abiding trust in God that was constructed on God's unconditional love for them. But what made this covenantal relationship radical was that trust in God carried with it an unconditional commitment to each other. The covenant, symbolized by the blood Moses splashed on the altar and sprinkled on the people, captured the unique relationship between God and the people. The blood of the covenant made them a holy nation. They were God's special people and were to treat each other with the same quality of reverence they gave to God.

The blood of Jesus which seals the new covenant between God and us expresses this new relationship in the language of love: "Love one another as I have loved you" (Jn. 15: 12). Jesus goes on to tell his disciples the limits of this love: "Greater love has no one than this, that one lay down one's life for one's friends" (Jn. 15: 13).

Many years ago I read about a young couple in Chicago who brought to life the reality of this kind of love. In 1976, a young man named Peter was severely injured in a car accident. His brain was damaged, and the doctors told Peter's family that he probably would not survive. Even if he did, the doctors said, he would always be in a comatose state. One of the people who heard that frightening diagnosis was Linda, Peter's fiancee. In the days following the accident, Linda kept vigil at Peter's bedside. She held his hand, patted his cheek, rubbed his brow, talked to him. All the while Peter remained in a coma, unresponsive to Linda's loving presence. Day after day for three and a half months, Linda sat with Peter. She spoke words of encouragement to him even though he gave no indication that he heard her.

Then one night, Linda saw Peter's toe move. A few nights later, she saw his eyelash flutter. Linda continued to encourage Peter. She massaged his arms and his legs as if her touch would bring his motionless limbs back to life. After many more months, the day came when Peter spoke his first word since the accident. It was only a grunt but it was the most beautiful word Linda had ever heard. Gradually, with Linda's help, those grunts turned to clear words. Two years after the accident, Peter and Linda were married. Peter was able to speak slowly, but clearly, his commitment of love to Linda.

In Linda's unconditional love for Peter during those days and months after the accident and in the years of rehabilitation, we see the true meaning of Jesus' challenge to love one another and the true nature of covenant. It means loving even at the risk of losing, caring at the risk of ridicule, speaking when the other seems not to hear, touching when there is no response, hoping in the smallest signs of life, having courage when fear and weariness and loneliness seek to overwhelm. The love of Jesus teaches us how to dream when all we see is death.

In a word, love means commitment. To be committed to the other, to other human beings, to all that God has made, to be committed with a passion, a purpose and a power that is not one's own but is the love of God, the blood of Christ, pulsing within us.

The conspiracy of compassion calls us to this quality of love. Our breathing together beckons us to ask some very difficult and dangerous questions that test the quality of our love. Questions like:

Am I willing to go to the limits of love taught to us by Jesus, and to go to those limits for anyone?

Am I willing to speak when no one seems to hear, to listen when words are left unspoken but pain is etched in another's eyes, to touch someone with hope and compassion when I am caught in the grip of despair, to love even when the losses keep mounting?

How can we learn such love if we do not learn it from one another — from listening to one another's memories and stories and dreams? I don't know where we can learn such love except from our ancestors — our grandmothers and grandfathers, our mothers and fathers, mentors and teachers — who have meant so much to us not because of the accumulation of their accomplishments but because of the quality of their commitments.

Refreshing Our Memory

Our breathing together is based on this covenant of love which has the power to resist and ultimately to conquer the forces of evil. The film *Weapons of the Spirit* gives us a good example of how this conspiracy can happen and suggests a vital ingredient in making it happen: the power of memory. The film tells the little-known story of Le Chambon, a village in the south of France whose residents sheltered thousands of refugees fleeing the Nazis. The citizens of this small town, which was comprised mostly of poor farmers, hid, fed and housed thousands of Jews seeking to escape Hitler's Holocaust.

The film documents how the town helped these people on their way to freedom from the Nazis; it contains interviews with many who were given sanctuary in Le Chambon and with villagers who opened their doors to those on the run. "There were scattered individuals who did this sort of thing everywhere in Europe, of course," one woman said. "But this was an entire community effort...by people so poor they had almost nothing to share but shared it all anyway — and risked everything to do so. I never heard of that happening anywhere else."

According to those interviewed in the film, 5,000 Jews found sanctuary in this tiny village. "They risked their lives," one of the people who found refuge in Le Chambon said. "It was an unimaginable outburst of solidarity."

One of those who opened her doors to the Jewish refugees said, "It happened quite naturally. We can't understand the fuss. I helped simply because they needed help."

This "natural" expression of compassion, love and courage by the citizens of Le Chambon was rooted in their own memories of persecution. Le Chambon was a community that had been settled by devout Huguenots. Their ancestors had fled their own persecution some 300 years before. And the children of these refugees had not forgotten.

The difference was memory — the people of Le Chambon remembered the agony of their ancestors. The people of this small village in the mountains risked their own lives to save others from deportment and certain death. They remembered, and in this marriage of memory and compassion, courage was born and given a name: Le Chambon.

At one point in the book of Exodus when God, through Moses, outlines the ramifications of the covenant for the people, we read: "You shall not wrong a stranger or oppress him, for you were once strangers in the land of Egypt" (Ex. 22: 21). God, who adds, "I am compassionate," seems to be saying, "Let me refresh your memory! Don't you remember Egypt?" Memory becomes a powerful motivation for compassion. Our service to others is based in part on our ability to remember.

Sometimes it seems, however, that we suffer from amnesia. We fail to recall those God moments, those memories when God's gracious love has erupted in our lives. We fail to feel our own wounds when we are confronted with those who are suffering. When confronted with obstacles, we don't recall how we survived them in the past with the help of God's grace. When confronted by people with whom we have difficulty, people with whom we disagree, people whose faults are obvious to us, we have a short memory regarding our own limitations and weakness. When tempted to deny hospitality or hope to another, we fail to remember that we too were once strangers, that we too once felt despair, that we too have gone unnoticed or unwanted. Recent efforts to change immigration policies and close the borders of the United States to those seeking refuge and a new beginning in the "land of the free" seem to be a direct result of our amnesia about our own heritage as a nation of immigrants.

On a personal level, I recall one Saturday morning when I was sitting in my study at the rectory going over my notes for my homily that evening and the doorbell rang. I ran downstairs and peeked through the window before opening the door. There he stood, another transient, the third one in the past couple of days. He was relieving himself in the bushes as his eyes scanned the rectory.

I invited him into my office. He took out an empty pack of cigarettes that were stuffed with butts he had picked up off the street. Carefully he squeezed the tobacco from four or five and put it on a slip of cigarette paper. "Times are tough," he said.

It was early spring and people were on the move again. The warmer weather brought people like this man out onto the streets. He was out of work, homeless and looking for a bus ticket to the city where perhaps he could find a job. "I'm not looking for a handout," he told me. But in the back of my mind the specter of an old stigma reared its ugly head: This man was frisking my pockets, looking for loose change. If he found some from me, he would move on to the next church or maybe the next town in search of another gullible minister.

I told him I would pay for his ticket and take him down to the bus station. So I made the arrangements, and when I hung up the phone, this weary warrior of the road knelt down and asked if I would hear his confession. His humility unmasked my self-righteousness. We celebrated the sacrament of reconciliation and I knew then that I should have been the one kneeling, asking for his forgiveness.

Later that morning as he stepped on the bus, he turned to shake my hand. A simple gesture so easily taken for granted, and yet at that moment he gave me a sign of peace. In his slight smile of gratitude, he gave me grace. In his gentle way of good-bye, he gave me his blessing.

That gentle pilgrim passing through town reminded me that we are all connected in a covenant of love. He released me for a moment from my amnesia, showing me again how God comes to us in various disguises — sometimes as a broken man on the front porch of a rectory looking for help and hospitality.

Jesus makes it simple for us. In his command to love, he condenses all the written and unwritten rules of the covenant into two basic principles: Love God and love your neighbor. If we really understand and embrace the depth of God's love for us; if we feel in every fiber of our flesh and bones the power of how that love was expressed in the most dramatic example of God's memory, the death and resurrection of Jesus, then we cannot help but live this Spirit of love. And when we do, our lives are characterized by gratitude and memory.

The Fire of Love

The memory of our own wounds motivates us to heal and give hope, to reconcile and to remember, to believe and to proclaim that God is with us always. Fragile though we are at times, fidelity to that vision is what matters most. Weak and weary though we are at times, we are never to relinquish the dream. Though at times we are unknowing about how to love, we are never to abandon the hope that guides our future. This future is captured in the words of Teilhard de Chardin: "Someday," he wrote, "after mastering the winds, the waves, the tides, and gravity, we shall harness for God the energies of love. And then, for the second time in the history of the world, we will discover fire."

Our conspiracy of compassion with Christ calls us to awaken each other from our coma of contentment with the passion of our God. We are to have fire in our bellies and fire in our bones, fire in our hearts and fire in our homes. We are not to be satisfied with the way things are but are called to see what the world might be, or what our families might be like, if we were ever to unleash the energies of love. We do this by being committed, deeply, passionately committed, to the way of love lived by Jesus. Such love has the power to wash our weary world of the stain of sin; the power to quench the parched lives of those who thirst for justice and peace; the power to reconcile those broken by infidelity and redeem those lost in fear; the power to liberate the lives of the poor and abandoned; the power to comfort those who are desperate and dying; the power to heal the wounds of our spouses, children, parents, co-workers, wounds that the world has inflicted or that we have inflicted on each other; the power to create families and communities in which people pour out themselves for each other.

This is the conspiracy Christ initiated, the covenant of love he reclaimed. It has the power to make us and our world young again. When we remember God's compassion toward us, we know we are people of life, not death; of courage, not fear; of commitment, not caution. And our lives will "bear fruit" and our "fruit will abide" (Jn. 15: 16).

If we live in this way, as Jesus lived for the disciples, as Linda lived for Peter; as the people of Le Chambon lived for the victims of the Holocaust, then we shall come to know one more thing about this covenant of love with our God and with each other. We shall know joy: "These things I have spoken to you, that my joy may be in you, and that your joy may be full" (Jn. 5: 11).

Prayer: The Center of Community

As people seeking to create communities of compassion, prayer is at the center of our conspiracy. Prayer teaches us compassion because it makes us one with God and affects our relationships with each other. Like the cross, prayer is not only vertical; it is also horizontal. How we pray affects how we perceive the world around us.

We are often asked to pray for others and sometimes we may feel like Moses in that story from Exodus when he held up his hands during the battle (Ex. 17: 8-13). As long as Moses held his arms in the air, reaching toward heaven, the Israelites were successful; when his arms grew tired and fell to his side, the people were in trouble.

Our arms may grow weary holding the sick, the tired, the lonely, the poor, the bereaved, the outcast, the broken, the stranger, the victim in our prayerful arms and in God's loving presence. But in prayer, we are not asking God to change the conditions of the world that cause so much suffering. Rather, we are allowing God to freely enter our lives, to fill us with the courage we need not to relinquish compassion, to fill us with the strength and vision we need to bring our little corner of creation into a rhythm of breathing that reflects God's reign.

In our prayer together, we seek to enlarge the spaces of hope within us by allowing God's voice to stretch our hearts, our minds and our imaginations. In the solitude of our praying hearts and in the solidarity of a praying community, God's Spirit makes us inclusive rather than exclusive of others' pain and sorrow; generous rather than greedy in our love and compassion for others; open rather than closed to the possibilities of peace. By parenting that hope in prayer; by expanding those places of hope within us, we offer the hospitality of hope to those lost in the darkness of despair.

Communal prayer nurtures creativity in us. When we are able to create an atmosphere of trust with those with whom we pray on a regular basis, we allow stories of our own experiences to spill out upon the floor. We reverence these tales of woe and wonder, and we realize there is very little we can *do* except *be* present to others.

And yet in listening to these stories and reverencing these moments of self-revelation, we can also begin to piece together ways to respond to the suffering we see but so often feel impotent to impact with our lives. These caring responses can gradually grow into a lifestyle by cultivating an attitude of prayer that moves outward into compassionate action.

Like Jesus, Buddha, another great author of compassion, offered us a new way of looking out from under our prayer and through the window to our world. He devised a patient, progressive process of cultivating compassion that grows into action. He suggested that we plant a new idea, water it and watch it grow into an action. Then we are to plant that action in the furrows of our life experiences and relationships. If we plant it again and again, we will watch it become a habit. We thus become addicted to acts of kindness and compassion. When we plant these acts over and over again in the rich, fertile soil of loving souls, we watch them grow into a lifestyle of living for others. Such is a style of life that plants in others' hearts goodness and truth. It touches the very image of God in the other. When such a lifestyle becomes a conspiracy, watch what happens: The harvest will be ready, and we will reap a destiny beyond our wildest, most outlandish dreams — a destiny of peace.

Imagine that.

By breathing together, we seek to allow the Spirit to reignite the spark of fire, of passion, in each one with whom we share the sacred space of community. It is this fire of love that will burn down the barricades of exclusivity and transform us into inclusive communities of compassion.

Fire in the Wind

The Prophetic Challenge
of Inclusivity

In forming communities of compassion, we depend upon prophets to call us back to the covenant of love. Prophets are people who blow on the embers of burned out dreams caused by our infidelity to the covenant. They seek to rekindle our memory, our passion and our hope by encouraging us to stretch our hearts until they reach a breaking point. With our hearts broken open by the force of the prophet's words and witness, we not only find more breathing room for ourselves and for those who have been standing outside the walls, but we also rediscover the fire of love.

We learn how important this sense of prophetic passion is for compassionate discipleship in Luke's Gospel (Lk. 12: 49-53). Jesus reminds his followers that the purpose of his mission is to kindle a fire upon the earth and in our hearts: "I have come to light a fire on the earth. How I wish the blaze were ignited" (Lk. 12: 49). But we recognize at the outset while the embers are still smoldering, before they are stirred into flame, how dangerous it is to play with fire. Such a brush fire of passionate purpose will alienate some and separate others: "Do you think I have come to establish peace on the earth?" Jesus asks. "I assure you, the contrary is true; I have come for division. From now on, a household of five will be divided three against two and two against three" (Lk. 12: 51-52). The point is clear: If you've expected the journey of compassion to be nice and polite, think again! Jesus is blunt in his description of how the prophetic role within the faith community — and the prophetic role the faith community plays within the larger society — will cause divisions even within one's own family. The prophet's role of heightening the awareness of the disciples about the ultimate goal, the in-breaking of the reign of God, will cause divisions even among the disciples. Likewise, when we seek to live with compassion, we should not be surprised by the conflicts and controversies we will experience. But over time, as we remain faithful to the covenant of love, our breathing together will create a strong enough wind to rouse this fire we feel in our collective hearts to burn down the barricades. This wildfire fueled by the force of our breathing together will burn away the debris of our past infidelities and prepare the ground for a new birth of compassion.

The conspiracy of compassion is ignited by Christ's baptism of fire. "I have a baptism to receive," Jesus says. "What anguish I feel till it is over!" (Lk. 12: 50). The quality of peace that Jesus denies coming to establish is not the peace we normally practice or seek to keep, not the kind of peace Jesus conferred on his followers, not Isaiah's image of the peaceful kingdom in which all peoples were included and lived in harmony. Until that vision is given birth in reality and he or she is baptized into it, there is anguish in the heart of the prophet. And bringing that vision of peace into reality involves conflict. In letting go of our need for a "comfortable" lack of conflict, we can maintain a clear sense of priority in our life's purpose. For when we experience the rupture of relationships or the severing of some family ties due to the passion of our belief, we run headlong and heart-first into the kinds of conflicts Jesus describes to his first followers.

Drawing Fire

When we study the prophets in the Hebrew Scriptures, we discover how their own baptism by fire fueled their passion that caught them in controversy. Jeremiah, for example, was thrown into a cistern for speaking God's truth (See Jer. 37). At the time of Jeremiah, cisterns were used as reservoirs for watering crops, providing drinking water and storing water when the land was under siege. But in this case, a cistern was used to imprison a prophet.

Reflecting on that cistern where Jeremiah was tossed because he was stirring up the people about their impending doom — the destruction of Jerusalem — and was discouraging the military who were expected to defend the city against enemy attack, we come to the uneasy conclusion that this is where prophets are often tossed. Indeed, it is almost mandatory for prophets to be thrown into the mud of miry cisterns now and then. It's part of the job description, the "fringe benefit" — the "benefit" of prophets who live on the fringe. This is because prophets are people who are knee-deep in the mud of their own experiences. They speak from the deep well we might call the soul and shout the truth they discover to anyone who will listen. And because they seek to live the truth they discover, they are often cast into cisterns, for the truth is hard to hear.

Jeremiah didn't place much value on being accepted by his peers or the powers-that-be. Instead, he spoke honestly the truth God commanded him to speak. In the soul of every prophet there is a dream that will not die. It is not so much a dream that would fulfill an individual's ambition but rather speaks of a peoples' destiny. The prophet usually suffers for the sake of this dream because dreams by their very nature startle us and wake us from our sleep. More often than not, a prophet's words shake the stuffing of the status quo right out of us. So the prophet expects this rejection and suffering because if a dream is worthy to see the light of day, the prophet knows it will exact a price.

Few if any of us would call ourselves prophets because most of us like to get along with others. We like to keep the peace, no matter how uneasy or unsettling or how compromising the peace might be. We want to be accepted, well thought of, well received. And though from time to time we might speak out on an issue and alienate a longtime friend, or challenge a racist joke at work or a sexist practice at church, or participate now and then in a demonstration that seeks to raise awareness of an excluded minority, still we have trouble with the idea that Jesus has come into the world not for peace but for division.

In a world as divided as ours, we pray for peace and wish it to hurry. But today we hear that true peace will never come without paying an exacting and demanding price. Sometimes that price is spending a fair amount of time knee-deep in the slime, mud and debris of our cistern-like soul.

What might surprise us is that if we spend time in the prophet's cistern and someone comes along who takes pity on us and rescues us, what they draw from the cisterns is not water but fire. Jeremiah's stay in the cistern was the time of his baptism by fire.

What this baptism by fire implies is that we are willing to be in the thick of life. We are willing to believe that peace is not the absence of conflict or controversy but the balanced presence of integrity, wholeness, compassion and justice. To achieve these ingredients of that ancient belief about Shalom, we are to stand as living torches, blazing campfires, raging infernos that will prepare the world for the rebirth of relationship.

For awhile, this attitude of passion about true peace may cause even higher barricades and deeper divisions. But the longer we remain faithful to this prophetic call that comes from God, the more we will find that these moments of conflict or months of controversy might just be our most creative opportunities. After all, wasn't God the most creative when confronted with the chaos? Did not the dark abyss give God the incentive to create the light?

A Prophet's Creative Response

One priest from my religious community who creatively responded to the challenge of being a prophet was Gary Jarvis. I saw his creativity at work when I served with Gary on our province's justice and peace committee. In 1985, Gary suggested that we lay the foundation for inviting our province to take a public stand and endorse the sanctuary movement. Writing in our newsletter, Gary sought to educate our members about sanctuary. "The act of extending sanctuary is first an act of compassion," he wrote. "In the name of God and with the voice of the prophets, the sanctuary movement has demanded that practices which consign persons to suffering and death must cease."

Gary's words stirred the embers within the members of our community. Some of these embers ignited into anger that he would propose that we take a stand against the established policies of our government. I remember well how fearful we were to even suggest that our members make such a prophetic and public stand. Because of our fear, at one point we tried to remove the proposal from our assembly agenda, thinking our province was not ready. But then Gary's creativity took hold of the members of the justice and peace committee and inspired us to overcome our fears.

His creative response was twofold. First, in making the presentation, Gary introduced to the members a young man from El Salvador named Jorge who had escaped the violence in his native land and was living in sanctuary with Gary at the time. Then Gary asked one of our most respected elder members who had ministered in South America for years to serve as Jorge's interpreter as he told his story of the violence inflicted upon his family. Jorge told us how he had a price on his head; how he could not return to his homeland because he had spoken out against injustice and how if he were to return he would almost certainly be killed.

Now we could put a name and a face to the pain and suffering we had been reading and hearing about. And because the elder, respected member of the province was standing with Jorge and with Gary, and was clearly moved by Jorge's story, other members who had been resistant to this proposal were moved as well. With only one dissenting vote, the province passed a resolution to support the sanctuary movement and those who opened their doors as places of refuge for people like Jorge.

A Prophet in our Midst

As we explore the prophet's role in this conspiracy of compassion, we are aware of the tensions that will inevitably arise when we first hear the truth the prophet speaks. When we are drawn into the fire of the conspiracy, rather than being afraid of these tensions we use them to respond with creativity to the barriers that arise in our becoming an inclusive, covenant community.

Still, our breathing together may become labored when we hear Jesus say that he has come not to establish peace but rather division. When Jesus says that his baptism by fire will cause "father to be split against son and son against father, mother against daughter and daughter against mother" (Lk. 12: 52), the moment of a breakdown of our most treasured family relationships may cause an anxiety attack, making it difficult to catch our breath. Take, for instance, the story of a young man named Jerry. His behavior was baffling to his parents. He got along with the children in the neighborhood with whom none of the other children played. When choosing sides for baseball, Jerry was often one of the first chosen. But the game was not allowed to begin unless all the kids — no matter whether they could hit or throw or run — were chosen. This was Jerry's plan: Everyone had to be included. His attitude caused some friction among the members of his team, but Jerry felt it was better to antagonize the whole team rather than ostracize one or two of the children.

At the dinner table, when his parents talked about the family that had moved in down the street, saying how "different" they seemed, Jerry said that their son was okay. "I don't want you playing with that boy," his father said.

But Jerry did anyway. And when the table talk came around to this particular family and Jerry's mother and dad talked about them in very negative terms, Jerry said, "Mom, Dad, I wish you wouldn't talk about my friends like that." An uneasy silence hung over the table for the rest of supper.

When Jerry grew into adulthood, he continued to question why some people were excluded, always left out, always on the outside looking in. Whether it was in college, or at work, or even at his church, there always seemed to be those who were on the fringe, unable to find a place at the center of anyone's concern or attention.

Because of where he stood, Jerry soon became an outsider himself. He was no longer invited to parties because he would always bring along someone who wasn't invited. The boss stopped asking him to important meetings at work because he would always raise an issue that made everyone else uncomfortable. And even at his church, his pastor asked him to resign from the church council because Jerry was always challenging official teachings of the church or questioning the authority of the pastor and council in some of their decisions.

It wasn't long before Jerry's reputation preceded him wherever he went. He was labelled a troublemaker who had problems with authority. Though a few folks admired how Jerry spoke his mind and his passion for the underdog was certainly obvious, most thought of him as an arrogant activist on an ego trip who was not interested in the welfare of the group but in tearing it apart.

In his quiet moments when he was alone — which was often since his blunt manner and fiery personality put others off — Jerry wondered why he was like this. Was he born with this instinct which we have described as prophetic? An image he used to explain his intense passion for those not included was that of sitting before a fire. As the fire rages in the fireplace, the fire consumes the logs, creating sparks and smoke. But every now and then, a log or a piece of wood falls away from the fire. By itself, away from the heat of the blaze, this piece of wood grows cold.

The fire is God and we are the logs. Away from the fire of community, apart from the heat of our common passion, we too grow cold. The goal of the compassionate life is to catch fire, to be on fire with love, with God. That is why Jerry's life became like a furnace, too bright for some, too hot for others, but always leading him to stand with those who for whatever reason had fallen away or been pushed away from the fire of community. Sometimes it was the color of their skin or the content of their creed. Sometimes it was their economic situation or honest disposition. Sometimes it was their sexual orientation and sometimes their gender-inclusive proclamations. And sometimes it was simply because they were "different," however that was defined at a particular time, in a particular place, by a particular group.

No matter how much Jerry wanted to be accepted by his peers, welcomed by his family, included by his colleagues and approved by his church, Jerry's passion was fueled by the belief that Jesus had come to light a fire on the earth and longed for it to be ignited. It was only when Jerry accepted himself, particularly the prophet within him, that he was able to appreciate how he served the whole community. He was able to see how he could fuel the fire of the conspiracy, how he could help the community plunge beneath the surface of their collective wounds to a place where healing could take place in the breath of the Spirit.

Again, unlike Jerry, most of us seek peace at any price. We house-train our prophets as we would our pets; otherwise, like Jerry and Jeremiah, Gary and Jesus, they create such a mess. Since prophets are difficult to domesticate, they learn to live outdoors, by campfires, in cisterns and under porches. And every now and then, they climb onto our porches and shout to us, "Come out, come out, wherever you are."

The prophet understands instinctively what we have been saying about this conspiracy of compassion: that the way to glory is through suffering, not around it or over it. And what do we gain by going through this painful process of living this truth? Maybe we live more honestly, with a hope that does not depend on results. Maybe we live more compassionately, with a peripheral vision for those on the fringe. Maybe we live more simply, with fewer constrictions imposed by societal and ecclesial norms. Maybe we live more consistently, with not so many compromises to our core beliefs.

The consequences of remaining faithful to the prophetic role this conspiracy calls us to are frightening: Expect rejection, alienation, to be silenced at times by religious authorities, and maybe even to merit the crown of martyrdom. Like Jerry, expect to find that we are often on the outside looking in. But from this vantage point, we pitch our tent with some of God's favorite people: the ones who know their own pain, who have plunged or been pushed into the fiery furnace of transformation. When we emerge from this immersion in fire, we are purified.

Prophets are often thrown into the fire. Their destiny, and ours, is to catch fire, to become the fire — and so to warm the cold, dark night with the radiance of God's redemption and compassion. There is a Swahili song which says, "Life has meaning only in the struggle. Triumph or defeat is in the hands of God, so let us celebrate the struggle." Prophets embrace this belief that the struggle for reconciliation among peoples and an inclusive community characterized by compassion is what gives meaning to their lives.

We now turn to another prophet, Isaiah, to learn how though our breathing together might become labored because of rejection, we can still celebrate the struggle.

Celebrating the Struggle

Isaiah's call to be a prophet is reminiscent of the scene from *The Wizard of Oz* when Dorothy and her companions are granted an audience with the great wizard. Remember how the fierce face projected from a cloud of smoke drives them to their knees in fear and homage. For Isaiah, "the foundations of the thresholds shook...and the house was filled with smoke." The scene is awesome and mysterious, with "God sitting upon a throne, high and lifted up; and his train filled the temple." Isaiah hears seraphim singing the ancient hymn that has become so familiar: "Holy, Holy, Holy is the Lord of Hosts! they cried to one another. All the earth is filled with God's glory!" (Is. 6, 1-8).

As Dorothy, Scarecrow, Tin Man and the Cowardly Lion found the courage to do the improbable by retrieving the witch's broom, so Isaiah's close encounter with God allows him to do the impossible: He becomes a prophet to the nations. The story reminds us that it is the glory of God that takes us beyond our human limitations and allows us to ride on the wings of new courage. This encounter with God establishes the quality of faith that frees us to love even when our shoulders are weighed down with grief or our stomachs knotted with fear. Such faith encourages us to keep our hope alive in the midst of the struggle.

This song of praise, "Holy, Holy, Holy," echoed at every Mass sets the stage for Isaiah's call to conversion. But notice how Isaiah approaches this "holy of holies" with fear and trembling: "Woe is me! For I am lost; for I am a man of unclean lips, and I dwell in the midst of a people of unclean lips." How easily we recite or sing the Holy, Holy, Holy at Eucharist. How readily those words flow from our lips. And yet they are the sound of the trumpet that ushers us into the most sacred space of our lives. Do we proclaim those words with an intensity and fervor as if they are leaping from an awesome encounter with the Divine Mystery? Or have they become dulled by repetition?

Listen to what Isaiah says: He is doomed because his sins of speech have rendered him unclean. He is unworthy to sing the anthem of praise to God. We too are scarred by the sins of our speech. Our tongues are at times like sharp swords that unleash violence upon others. Our words cut through egos and reputations, leaving them bruised and bleeding. We use our tongues to condemn and to gossip, to scold and to criticize; to lay waste and plunder the dignity of other human beings. Our lips have allowed devastation and destruction to pass through the gates of our mouths. Certainly we can identify with Isaiah in his desire to turn back. But we can also resonate with the sentiment of the centurion whose words we say before receiving the body and blood of Christ: "Lord, I am not worthy to receive you, but only say the word and I shall be healed."

Acknowledging before God his unworthiness, Isaiah says boldly, "My eyes have seen the King, the God of Hosts." This is grace. Pure grace. Amazing grace. Unworthy though he is, Isaiah is given a vision of God's throne, God's majesty, God's love.

Then the moment of truth arrives: "Then flew one of the seraphim to me, having in his hand a burning coal which he had taken with tongs from the altar." The image is striking: The altar is ablaze — a furnace of love. It is the place of redemption. The altar is a raging fire kindled by the mercy of God. Bring here the sin of our lives, the fear that imprisons us, the guilt that haunts us, and with Isaiah watch what happens: "He touched my mouth with (the burning ember) and said: 'Behold, this has touched your lips; your guilt is taken away, and your sin forgiven.'" Cleansed from sin, Isaiah's energy is inflamed by the fire from the altar of God's love. His lips now burn with truth. Isaiah is ready. Indeed, all his senses have been awakened: "I heard the voice of the Lord saying, 'Whom shall I send, and who will go for us?' Then I said, 'Here am I! Send me.'"

The call of Isaiah and ours is the same: To be holy as our God is holy. Our close encounter with God at the altar of reconciliation awakens our senses to the reality of God's presence in all those places in our world where human beings are consumed not by the fire of love but by loneliness and longing, grief and greed. In the midst of the struggle to bring those who are outside the circle of community into the fire of our love, to stand at the altar of our reconciliation, we recognize that this altar of God's redeeming love is found not only in a church. This altar can be anywhere: in schools or on street corners, in coffee shops or confessionals, in paneled board rooms or steel-cage prison cells. For me, it was profoundly experienced around a table in the senior citizen's activity center in Centerville, Iowa.

A Close Encounter with God

St. Mary's in Centerville was my first assignment as a priest. Soon after I arrived, I was talking with the social concerns committee of the parish about the economic situation of the town and area. We discussed ways we could help the poor in the community. One idea that surfaced was to start a soup kitchen. Now Centerville is not a large city, so we realized we were not talking about the kind of daily soup kitchen that has become so prevalent and necessary in urban areas where the homeless population continues to increase. But being in a rural area that had felt the impact of farm foreclosures and with a large number of elderly on fixed incomes, we felt there was a need to do something. So we decided to sponsor a Saturday Free Lunch at the local senior citizens activity center to help people who might need to stretch their budgets. A free meal or two might help their money go a little farther.

One of the people who came regularly was Jimmy, a fifty-year-old man who spent his days scavenging through parking lots, ditches and gutters in search of aluminum cans. (In Iowa at the time, there was a five-cent refund for each aluminum can.) Jimmy was well-known in town simply as the "Can Man." He pulled his cart along the streets and I had seen him often, but I never knew him until he started coming to the free lunches.

Jimmy was thin and hunchbacked; his face long and narrow, with wrinkled, leathery skin stretched across high cheekbones. His dark, deep-set eyes had a hungry look.

That first Saturday Jimmy must have put away three or four bowls of soup and countless pieces of bread. We were amazed by how much food he could put into his frail body. But as much as he ate week after week, the food was not the real reason Jimmy came to the soup kitchen. Jimmy enjoyed being with the people who gathered there on Saturday afternoon. It was a community of people, some down on their luck, others just enjoying the companionship, sharing their stories of what happened during the week. They ate a simple meal of bread and soup and gradually began to share their lives, which, even though they had tasted pain, were still brimming with hope.

Jimmy and the others were like the Israelites wandering in the desert. However, instead of grumbling because of the lack of food, they seemed to understand what Moses meant when he said, "One does not live by bread alone, but by everything that proceeds out of the mouth of God" (Dt. 8: 3). The streets of a small town in Iowa were Jimmy's desert. Like the Israelites, he knew what it meant to be hungry and thirsty, but also like our ancestors in faith, he knew what it meant to depend on God for his very survival. He knew, too, what it meant to rely on the kindness of strangers — people who were not strangers for very long because they broke the bread of friendship together.

Being with Jimmy and the others on those Saturday afternoons in Centerville taught me much about Eucharist and about how to celebrate in the midst of struggle. Whether gathered around an altar table in church or a folding table at the senior citizens' center or a family kitchen table, we stand on the threshold of transformation. The bread we break and the wine we pour, which become the body and blood of Christ, invite us to partake of a meal of memory where our God shares divine life with us. We come to the altar to allow Christ to erase our amnesia and to restore our memory of the very life that God promises us: "The one who eats my flesh and drinks my blood abides in me, and I in him" (Jn. 6: 56).

This holy communion in the furnace of friendship is the feast of forever, where we share the cup of blessing and break the bread of our companionship. It also reflects the experiences of our ancient ancestors in faith. They received bread from heaven — manna — as they journeyed across the wilderness. The Eucharist provides us with our bread from heaven — our communion with God through Jesus, who comes into our bodies and creates in our hearts a longing for love, for unity, for joy, as we continue our pilgrim way across the daily desert of routine.

When I think back on those Saturday afternoon lunches in Centerville and remember Jimmy, I can still see his eyes longing for more than the soup and sandwiches we offered. His stomach was filled, but something much more important was happening: His spirit was nourished as he found love in the company of friends.

That is the invitation and challenge of every Eucharist: To celebrate the struggle as God rekindles the spark of our desire for reconciliation. It is the invitation to gather in the company of friends to share the stories of a loving God who takes us by the hand and teaches us the way of compassion. We break bread and pour wine, and so Jesus is intimately united with us, and we with each other. The challenge, then, is to go forth as people who remember. We go forth as people whose hearts are filled with hope and memory and joy so that we might break the bread of friendship with the Jimmys of our lives. In doing so, we discover how the circle of our companionship grows so wide that no one is left standing outside.

The Desire To Serve

Our desire to serve the Jimmys of our world is sparked at the table in our companionship with others. When our sense of sin has been purged and our senses have been opened, we respond to God's invitation to be altars of sacrifice and tables of reconciliation. Worthiness or unworthiness is not at issue in the discernment of God's will and our call to be prophet: We are all unworthy. The question is one of desire. Are we willing to stand before the altar, aflame with love? Are we willing to stand close enough so that its heat singes our skin and its embers shoot like stars upon our bodies?

"Don't stand too close to the fire" is sensible advice except when what is on fire is God. Just ask Moses.

Our God wishes to set us ablaze with love. It is a desire to go forth as flashing flames to burn away the rubble of sin and decay, to make the ground ready for a new birth, a new creation that will emerge from the ashes.

Isaiah learned how dangerous it is to play with fire. He stood too close, and God reached out and touched him. Purified by God's glowing embers, Isaiah responded to the call to be prophet and raced from the altar to set the world afire with God's love. I got too close to Jimmy and his eyes burned a hole in my soul.

Each of us has encountered this mystery of our faith more than once in our lives. We may have learned it in the fidelity of our parents or grandparents, in our family, from our friends or from ancestors in community. We may have experienced it in the forgiveness of an injury. It might have come to us in the silence of prayer or in the joyful noise of a crowd. We may have seen it in the faces of the poor or in the eyes of a starving child. We may have heard it in the words of an orator or the melody of a favorite song. We may have welcomed it in the kindness of a stranger or the warm embrace of a forgotten friend.

For Isaiah, it came in the embers of a blazing altar. For me, it came from a Can Man. But however it comes, when it comes, we know we will never be the same again.

A Prophet's Death: Transforming Community

I saw how this encounter with the Divine Mystery can begin to transform a community in the death of the prophet I spoke of earlier, Gary Jarvis. In death as in life, Gary's spirit prophetically ignited the fire of compassion. Gary died in 1988 at the age of 37. His death at such a young age deeply affected the members of the province. The cause of his death, AIDS, confronted us with a disease that many of us had been fleeing from with a fear fueled by ignorance. Gary's death brought the reality of AIDS home and caused a multitude of reactions and emotional responses. But the most dangerous response was silence. Not to allow Gary's life and death to move us and change us and mold us would have been a tragic mistake. To continue to be numb or indifferent to the pain and suffering this disease causes would have appeased fear and encouraged ignorance to prevail.

But, as happens in many families, a death in our religious family changed us. During the two years following Gary's death, members of the province met in small groups to discuss an AIDS policy proposed by the provincial council. The process mattered more than the policy. We became more aware of HIV and AIDS, more compassionate, more sensitive. Far more important than the words of the policy statement were the words that were spoken in those small group meetings. Words formed not only in the head but in the heart. Words heard not only with reason but with respect and reverence. Words often breathed in pain or doubt or confusion led to a breathing together, a conspiracy toward compassion. And so Gary's death taught us what Gary's life tried to teach us: how to care and how to love the outcast, the stranger, the poor, the oppressed, the victim.

This was an experience of how the paschal mystery can fashion a future full of hope. The tragedy of Gary's death brought new life, a new understanding. We cannot anticipate such experiences, but when they do invade the circle of community, we must be willing and ready to respond with a love born of the covenant. We must be willing to risk the fear of disclosure and surrender to the dream of our destiny: "Love one another as I have loved you." We must be ready to trust enough to say what we think, willing to feel enough to love even those with whom we disagree.

By sharing and reflecting on a common story, by drinking from a common cup of suffering, we are forever changed. Our lives so affected that whenever forces of fear seek to constrict our hearts, whenever indifference seeks to smother compassion, whenever patience wears thin or pride bursts forth, the prophetic spirit is there to enlarge us, to extend us, to expand us. Gary's prophetic life and death have been for me vivid invitations to be more compassionate, more patient, more humble — and more passionate in making the reign of God a reality in our day.

Hope in our future lives and breathes on our memories of the past with all its pain and promise. Our willingness to share our stories in the sacred space of our family's sanctuary and in the collective stirring of our common life leads us to and flows from the tables of reconciliation where we gratefully recall God's presence and action in our lives.

Companionship at the table of the Lord not only reminds us of our redemption as we remember the passion and death of Jesus, it can also be the action that changes our lives. In the company of those we love, cowardly spirits become courageous and timidity gives way to tenacity in living Gospel values.

As we gather around the table of the Eucharist, we bring with us all those people we represent: the ones with whom we live and work; our family and friends with all their struggles, setbacks and suffering; the poor ones who cry out to us as we pass them on the street; the lonely ones whose sighs never quite reach our ears. Here at the altar aflame with God's love our senses are opened, and we see how the lives of the poor and outcast are intimately connected with our own. We hear their cries and sighs in between the lines of sacred truth proclaimed. We taste their pain and ours, forever transformed in the chalice where we "share in the divinity of Christ who humbled himself to share in our humanity."

In each Eucharist, we bring to the table all the sorrow and pain we claim; all the doubts and fears to which we cling, all the sin and death that seek to stifle our spirit. We place them on the table and in the cup and see them transformed into the very life of God.

Here is the real moment of reconciliation — for here is where eternity touches time, where heaven engages earth, where divinity mingles with humanity. It is here, even in the midst of our suffering, our eyes downcast in self-pity, that we are invited to look to the coming of the reign of God.

At every Eucharist, we encounter the real presence of Christ — first in the community gathered in prayer and then in the bread and wine that have become the body and blood of Jesus — and so are challenged to be the real presence of Christ in the world. This divine blood transfusion gives us the courage to pour out our lives in loving service of others as we seek to give our world a glimpse of our destination: the redemption won for us by Christ.

But how do we sustain this prophetic sense of reconciliation after we have left the table of the Lord and the community of the faithful? How does God call us from the complacency that so often consumes us to the conspiracy of compassion we celebrate in the breaking of the bread? How does God move us from a sense of sin to a sense of solidarity with all God's creatures and all of creation? What happens when the fire of love we feel inside burns low because of rejection or lack of results? The next chapter will explore these questions as we address an ailment that for many in our world has reached epidemic proportions: compassion fatigue.

Holding Our Breath

Cures for Compassion Fatigue

There are times in our lives when the fire of compassion we feel inside burns low or even dies out. This experience has become known in our culture as "burnout" or "compassion fatigue." But it is not a new disease. As we shall see, the first victims of this illness were Adam and Eve. Many of the prophets, most notably Elijah, were afflicted with compassion fatigue. Like any illness, before we can find a cure we must know the cause. Actually, there a number of contributing factors, but the following story gives us a clue about one of the chief causes of compassion fatigue:

Ralph owned a beautiful red sports car. It was the envy of the neighborhood. A colleague at work, Frank, often asked Ralph about selling the car. Ralph always politely refused. But Frank was obsessed with this car. He offered Ralph five times what the car was worth, but Ralph always declined, saying he was very attached to the car and didn't want to sell it.

Frank's obsession became so great that he decided to get the car by any means that he could. One night he was driving down a country road that he knew Ralph used on his way home from work. Frank found a spot where there was a steep incline, got out of his car, released the emergency break and pushed his car over the cliff. Then, being very careful — since he really didn't want to get hurt but only appear to be hurt — he rolled down the hill himself.

Shortly after this staged accident, Ralph came driving along the same road in his red sports car. He noticed some smoke coming up from the side of the hill. Stopping his car, he went to the side of the cliff. There he saw a car and somebody lying motionless beside it. He hurried down the embankment. When he discovered it was his friend, Frank, he carried him up the side of the hill, placed him in his sports car and rushed him to the hospital.

Because Frank's injuries were not serious, he was released immediately after undergoing a few tests. But his car was totalled. Ralph offered to give Frank a ride home. On the way, he said, "You know, Frank, I've been thinking. You've been wanting to buy this sports car for a long time. And now that you don't have a car of your own, I've decided to give you this one."

Frank was astounded. "You're going to give me your car?"

"That's right," Ralph said. "In fact, why don't I drive to my house, and then you can take the car home." Frank could not believe his ears. His plan had worked better than he thought. He had hoped Ralph would feel sorry for him and offer to sell him the car. But now he was going to give it to him! And that's just what Ralph did: He gave Frank his prized red sports car.

Several weeks later, guilt began to get the best of Frank. He decided to be honest with Ralph and to give him back the car. He told Ralph about staging the accident as a way to tap Ralph's sympathy. Ralph listened and then said, "Keep the car, Frank. I only ask one thing: that you never tell this story to anyone else as long as you live."

"Of course," Frank said. "But why?"

"Because every day people come upon accidents and many other desperate situations. If your story became known, some may think that an accident they encounter has been staged or that a person who is begging really isn't poor or desperate but is only using them. And they will not stop to help."

One of the causes of compassion fatigue is having our good intentions and actions exploited or used by another who really doesn't need our help. Remember in the Good Samaritan story how the priest and Levite hurried by the person who had been robbed and beaten. Perhaps they were suffering from Compassion Fatigue Syndrome (CFS). Perhaps they had stopped and helped others before but felt they had been unappreciated or that their compassion had been abused. So now they felt, "What's the use?"

But the Samaritan broke the cycle of CFS with a pain reliever comprised of a simple ingredient: the knowledge of self. Because he knew who he was — an outcast himself, accustomed to life on the fringe, aware of his own wounds caused by his alienation — he was able to break the cycle of CFS by stopping to help the one who had been victimized by thieves. When the grace of God infiltrates our system to remind us of our true identity that we are to be "compassionate as our God is compassionate," and when we embrace this identity, we are more likely to respond with compassion when others seek to harm us or hurt us. We will be true to our identity even when others hate us and take from us, even when others seek to destroy us. We know who we are, and nothing the other does to us can ever diminish or demolish our true self. We know who we are. We are compassionate as our God is compassionate.

Memory Creates a Soft Heart

Knowledge of who we are is influenced by those experiences in our lives which have taught us the meaning of compassion. When we keep these memories alive, we find a vital source of strength. These sacred anecdotes become like vitamins and minerals that will keep our hearts supple and soft, and so serve as essential antidotes to the virus of Compassion Fatigue Syndrome. If left unchecked, this virus creates hard hearts, and hard hearts crush compassion.

The power of such sacred stories is found in the experience of Father Bill. He had been a priest for fifteen years and was now quite content living in a small rural parish just off the interstate. The highway weaved through the lifeless landscape like a concrete stream. He had grown to like the small town, but it had taken a while to adjust. There were not so many interruptions here — especially from the "knights of the road" who used to knock at the rectory door at the large inner city parish where he spent the first years of his priesthood.

During those early years, Bill was awakened to the language and lifestyle of the street. Naive at first, he was often stopped by beggars looking for the legendary dime to buy a cup of coffee. He would carry change in his pocket to satisfy their caffeine fix. When people came to the door asking for a little help, Bill would go to the petty cash drawer in the safe and give them a couple of dollars. It didn't take long for the word to spread in the neighborhood that Fr. Bill was "generous." Perhaps "gullible" would have been a better adjective.

One day the pastor took his young associate aside because Bill's generosity was depleting the parish petty cash. The pastor had served more than thirty years in the city, and it had made his heart as hard as the sidewalks outside the church. He gave Bill a lecture on stemming the tide of poverty. "You know they are using the money you give them to buy booze or drugs or cigarettes," he said. "You're not helping them. On the contrary, you're contributing to their disease. You are making it more difficult for them to find a cure."

With the pastor's advice fresh in his mind, Bill soon began turning away those familiar faces that made a pilgrimage to his door. As he closed the door behind them and watched them walk down the steps, Bill knew in his head that the pastor was probably right, but in his heart there was an ache he could not dismiss. He knew he had to do something.

So he called a few friends in the parish and proposed the idea of starting a soup kitchen for the poor in the area. The idea was put into action a few weeks later in the cafeteria of the abandoned school. Because of the level of poverty and the number of people who had come to him for help, Bill expected the cafeteria to be filled. So he had some of the women make enough soup and sandwiches for one hundred. Ten people showed up. The small turnout confirmed for Bill that the pastor had been correct.

Disheartened, Bill felt used and cheated. He also discovered something else: The cement was starting to set in his heart.

As he helped clear the tables and mop the floor, Bill asked the volunteers to come back again tomorrow and try again. "But don't make so much soup," he told them.

After the volunteers had left, Bill sat alone amid the chairs piled up on the tables. He buried his head in his hands, unable to rid himself of the feeling of being played for the fool. Feeling sorry for oneself takes a lot of concentration, so Bill did not notice the old man with long, greasy gray hair come into the cafeteria. It was more his smell than the sound he made that finally awakened Bill from his trance of self-pity.

"Excuse me, sir," the old man said softly. "I heard I could get a bite to eat here." A toothless grin showed through the crease of his tangled beard.

Bill looked up and saw as ugly a man as he had ever seen. The dirt was caked on his brow, and his beard was matted down. He carried a stick in one hand, a shopping bag in the other. His green polyester suit and flowered shirt looked as if they were permanently pressed to his body.

"Uh, yes, but you're a little late," Bill said. "The cooks have already gone home, and the food is put away."

"Oh well, thank you anyway." The old man turned to leave.

"Wait," Bill said as he got up from the table. "I can get some soup and crackers for you. It'll only take a minute to warm up the soup."

"Thank you," the man said. "You are most kind." He set his bag down, took a chair off the table and sat down.

When Bill brought the old man his soup and crackers and an apple he found in the refrigerator, the old man's eyes opened wide and their brilliance seemed to burn away the dirt from his face. Bill set the food before him and turned to leave.

"Wait," the old man said gently. "Aren't you going to join me?"

"No, I'm afraid not. I've already eaten and I was just leaving when you came in. I have a lot of things to attend to over at the rectory."

But in a tone both inviting and demanding, the old man said, "Please, sit down."

Bill pulled out the chair and sat across from him. "Okay, but just for a moment."

He watched as the old man bowed his head. "Dear God," the old man said softly. "I thank you for this young man and the food he has placed before me. Bless this food, Lord, and bless this young man." Then he broke one of the crackers and said to Bill, "Please, I don't want to eat alone." He placed the cracker in Bill's open hand.

In breaking the bread of friendship and pouring the wine of celebration, we give of ourselves and receive so much more. The old man's simple gesture of breaking that cracker gave Bill the courage to go on. While the old man received a little soup, Bill received the spirit to continue sharing his life with others. And whenever Compassion Fatigue Syndrome causes his heart to harden, he remembers that old man and gives thanks for a soft heart.

Releasing the Devil's Grip

There are other causes for the feeling of fatigue to settle in our souls and cause us to be less compassionate. Recently I read of a breathing disorder known as acute pleurodyma, which is an inflammation of the chest cavity lining. Its symptoms include a sharp and sudden pain in the chest that lasts for a couple of days. The nickname for this disease is "devil's grip." Perhaps that is a good description of another cause of compassion fatigue; it's as if we are caught in the devil's grip.

Adam and Eve were the first to be diagnosed with "devil's grip." Remember the Genesis story of creation which says that God formed us out of the dust of the earth and blew into our nostrils the breath of life. This is original grace: God's breath gives us life. God's breathing in us allows us to live. But the story goes on to tell us that Adam and Eve, in the course of their unique and intimate relationship with God, took this gift of life, this original grace, for granted. They kept grasping for tempting opportunities that were within reach. Juicy fruits of fame, fortune and unlimited access to the comforts afforded by worldly success seduced them. They sensed their lungs, their lives, their egos being inflated. Pride, the original sin, took hold of Adam and Eve as their passionate pursuit of worldly goals kept them forever on the run, leaving them tired, exhausted, out of breath.

The story from Genesis suggests that in grasping to be gods, in setting themselves up as idols of their age, they ended up gasping for air. Adam and Eve's story is our story: How often do we think and act as if we can do this alone, that we don't need each other or don't have the time to care for another's needs. This is one of the root causes of compassion fatigue, and its worst symptom is that we don't have time or sense the need for God.

When our original sins replace the original grace of God's breath within us, the symptoms render a diagnosis of compassion fatigue. When we feel these symptoms, it is time to check our pulse and our priorities. It is time to slow down, to stop and listen to the heartbeat of God. It is time to seek some prayerful attention after we have fainted and fallen because of breathing in the pollution of pride that clouds our vision, stifles our spiritual capability and leaves us frail and pale.

The good news is that Compassion Fatigue Syndrome is curable. We can be released from the "devil's grip." A simple test will determine how serious our condition is and how advanced the disease has become in our lives. It's called the "desert treadmill test." It was first utilized by Moses and his team of specialists who wandered in the desert for forty years. They encountered many setbacks in overcoming their compassion fatigue — like the time they constructed that famous golden calf — and their frequent grumbling about not having enough food. But ultimately, with original grace gradually overtaking their original sins, the desert trimmed the fat of their inflated egos and made them fit to trust in God.

Jesus used this same treadmill test before he began his public ministry. In the process, he devised some new breathing exercises that are still useful today in combating compassion fatigue. By treading into the desert, Jesus offered us a regimen for getting back into spiritual shape.

Recall how Jesus was led out into the desert by the Spirit. On the treadmill, Jesus was tempted, and the temptations were tantalizing. Jesus, who had not eaten in days, was hungry. How tempting it would have been to turn that stone into a loaf of fresh-baked bread. He could probably smell the aroma and remember how his grandmother Anna's house used to smell after she baked bread. His mouth watered at the memory. But Jesus answered this temptation as he answered all the others: with the word of God. "Not on bread alone does one live." Jesus was hungry for holiness and would not allow the sweet temptation of fresh-baked bread to take his mind and his heart away from God. By resisting this temptation, Jesus began to breathe into the world the original grace of compassion.

The second temptation of Jesus was to make a spectacle and garner great fame. What a circus act it would have been to leap off the top of the temple. He could have flown through the air with the greatest of ease, and his name would have spread quickly throughout the land. But Jesus resisted and chose instead to fly with both feet on the ground. He chose to walk with us on the sometimes dusty path of life. He was and is a savior who is willing to enter fully the human experience through his suffering and death. By resisting the temptation to fame, the original grace of compassion finds even more room to breathe.

Finally, the third temptation was perhaps the most enticing of all: riches and power beyond measure. He could have had all the kingdoms of the world if only he had been willing to sell out his dream. The lure of such a lucrative contract was not tempting enough for Jesus who set his sights on only one kingdom: the kingdom of God. Jesus desired not to rule the kingdoms of the world but to usher in a new reign of peace and justice, love and truth — to unleash these values and virtues, this vision of hope upon the world. And now, finally, original grace had a face: the face of Jesus.

In combating this form of compassion fatigue in which we cannot find time for God nor sense our need for God, the recommended remedies are prayer, fasting and almsgiving. When we read the instructions on this spiritual medication, we discover how these remedies help us to breathe more freely by encouraging us to exhale those attitudes and actions that are self-centered and suffocating. They advise us to breathe deeply as we inhale the very breath of God.

On the desert treadmill, we begin to gain stamina for the long journey of compassion. When we go to the desert to breathe the fresh air of God's love, we are freed from the devil's grip that has filled our lungs with the stagnant and stale air of pride and prejudice. By spending time in the desert, we increase not only our lung capacity, but our life capacity — our ability to live and move in the rhythm of God's breathing.

Finding a Familiar Place

We also go to the desert to heal the symptoms caused by still another cause of compassion fatigue. When we feel overwhelmed by the wounds inflicted by life, or the lack of love, or the gradual realization that we will not achieve our dreams, or death or betrayal threatens to consume our commitment, we go to the desert to allow our wounds to breathe.

In August of 1987, two months after my brother Ed committed suicide, I went to his place at the Lake of the Ozarks, alone. Since Ed's death, no one else in the family had been to this place which for the last ten years of Ed's life had been his sanctuary from the storms of mental illness. He felt safe there but ultimately could never find the harbor of sanity he sought so desperately.

Ed's place at the lake was one of those spaces of solitude and silence that offered me an avenue of escape from the telephones and noise and appointments that made up most of my days when I was in parish work. When I moved to Sedalia, Missouri in July of 1985, I was only an hour or so from Ed's place. It was quiet there. Even if there were others enjoying the evening breeze in other cabins in the cove, they were unobtrusive. They came to escape too — to fish, to relax, to find that silent center that kept their worlds from unraveling. Once the trees blossomed in their new spring wardrobe, the place felt even more isolated. It was a perfect refuge from the fast pace, a shelter from the storm, an oasis from the intense heat that singed my time and burned away my days.

As I sat in Ed's cabin at the lake after his death, images of his life flooded my imagination: the fish he caught and mounted, the clothes hanging in the closet, even the calendar which still showed June, the last time any of the family had been at the lake. All these images tolled, in somber tones, Ed's memory. I stared at that Monday, June 8th, on the calendar — the day my brother died. In the solitude of Ed's place, with the water brushing gently against the shore, I found myself drawn to two stories from the biblical tradition: Elijah's encounter with God on the same holy mountain where Moses was called and Peter's encounter with Jesus during the storm at sea. Both spoke directly to the feelings that were whirling around inside my head and heart looking for a place to land. They landed in these passages, where I found a small measure of healing.

Picture Elijah being burned out and ready to throw in the towel (I Kgs. 19: 3-13). The weight of God's word has driven him to the edge. He is ready to buckle and bend and taste the dirt. He prays for death: "This is enough, O God! Take my life, for I am no better than my ancestors" (I Kgs. 19: 4). Elijah is suffering from extreme burnout. At one point in his life, Elijah had been on fire. He was passionate about proclaiming God's Word. Now, however, he is tired. The embers of his commitment are fading fast. So, with his enemies in hot pursuit, Elijah runs to the mountain of Horeb where he first encountered God, the place where the fire was first ignited.

After Ed's death, I was drawn to the place where during this life Ed was the happiest.

In his retreat to Horeb, Elijah finds God. But he finds God not in a burning bush or a strong wind or even a violent earthquake; Elijah discovers the divine in "a tiny whispering sound" (I Kgs: 19, 13), or as I've also heard it translated, "the sound of sheer silence." When he hears this sound, Elijah hides his face. But instead of cowering in the corner of the cave, Elijah goes and stands outside as if to catch this breath of God. It was this delicate touch in the silence and solitude that propels Elijah to continue the mission.

God comes to us when we least anticipate it and in ways that are far from expected. We so often attribute to God qualities of strength and power that we can miss God's gentleness. It is in this tender touch of the divine that the prophet is given the strength to continue his pilgrimage. In his weakness and fear he discovers that God reveals God's very self in a weak, faint whisper. But that is all Elijah needs to know that God is with him.

When loved ones die or dreams turn to dust and our inner resources have run out, we are afraid to go on. We wonder how we will ever continue. We worry if we will ever know joy again. But if we allow that still, small voice to crack through the wall of our fear, we will find in time the energy and the courage we need to go on.

In a story from the New Testament tradition, Peter finds the encouragement he needs that night during the storm when Jesus comes walking on the water to him and the other fearful disciples. Jesus comes to them out of solitude. As Mark tells the story in the sixth chapter of his Gospel, Jesus is exhausted after spending a long day preaching and teaching. As the crowds go home, he tells his companions to relax on the water, maybe do a little fishing, while he goes off by himself to pray. Jesus tries to steal a few hours of solitude. But after soaking in the silence, Jesus notices that the disciples are lost at sea in a raging storm. So he goes out to rescue them.

"He meant to pass by them," Mark writes (Mk. 6: 48). At first glance, those words seem to imply that Jesus is just going to walk on by. But the language conveys a sense of revelation — very much what Elijah experienced on the mountain when the prophet was told to "go forth, and stand upon the mount before the Lord...And behold, the Lord passed by" (II Kgs. 19: 11).

This story suggests that when we are lost at sea in the middle of our night, for healing to happen we must allow God to enter the pain. We must allow God to pass by us. By going in to the space of solitude, we take the risk to meet God halfway. But always remember that the closer we come to the peace God offers, the more fear will be there trying to get the best of us. It is then that God stretches out a hand to rescue us from drowning in despair.

Consumed by my own grief at the death of my brother, I went to the one sacred shrine in his life and came in touch with my own fear. My hope consumed, I was afraid to go on. But those few days gave me the courage to put Ed's life and death not in perspective but in a holy place. It was a space where I was able to sense in the whisper of the wind in the trees and the echo of the waves of the lake, the abiding presence of God.

Running on Empty

Where do we run when personal problems close in around us? Where do we run when death breaks into our safe and secure beliefs about life? Where do we run when the losses pile up and hope seems smothered at the bottom of the stack? Where do we run when anxiety sweeps through the open windows of our hearts leaving behind fear-like symptoms — chills, body ache, fever, loss of appetite? Where do we run when we don't know where we're going, and the gauge points to empty, and the darkness hovers over the horizon, and the road disappears? Where do we run when we are just too tired to go on, and weariness has wrapped our souls not with a *comforter* of a "job well done" but with a *discomfort* of doubt and worry as we wonder what difference we are making?

When we are running on empty because of personal problems or a terrible tragedy, because of loss of confidence or loss of friends, because of fears that get the best of us and worries that bring out the worst in us, we often run in the same direction Elijah and Jesus ran, in the direction of solitude. This is the place where we find our bearings, our belief, and maybe even our ability to hope again.

A few years ago I was giving a mission, a parish retreat, where I told the story about my brother Ed committing suicide and how I went to his place at the lake of the Ozarks by myself to try to ease the ache of this unacceptable loss. During the week of the mission, a young woman

I'll call Diane came to see me. She told how she could identify with why I had "run away" and wanted to be alone after my brother's death. She told me this story:

She and her brother Dave were only a couple of years apart. When they were children, they did everything together. They were precocious and charming; daring and sometimes delinquent. She smiled as she told me how her dad would come home from work and ask, "Well, how are my little scoundrels today?" They reveled in being "little scoundrels" who thought that no adventure was too daunting. Diane and Dave shared everything together when they were growing up, especially this appetite for adventure. There were no secrets between them. When they were in high school and Diane started dating, she always trusted Dave to tell her exactly what he thought about the latest boy she brought home. And Diane would tease her brother about the absence of a girlfriend in his life. "Dave was your typical tall, dark and handsome athlete, a real jock, whom every girl in school had a crush on," Diane said. "I would tease him about being so arrogant that he would never find a girl attractive enough for him."

Well, as Diane came to learn shortly after Dave graduated from high school, it wasn't arrogance that kept him from dating in high school. When Dave told her his secret — that he was gay — it didn't faze Diane in the least. "Why you little scoundrel," she told her brother. And then squeezing that appetite for adventure they shared, she teased: "So why didn't you ask the captain of the football team to the prom?" And they laughed at what a scene that would have caused in the small town where they were living.

It was then they both realized that there were some limits to their shared spirit of adventure. And with those limits, self-imposed or not, came a sense of fear neither one of them had known before.

But it wasn't until a few years later that both Diane and her brother Dave came to know the greatest fear of all: the fear to hope.

Diane recalled the night Dave called her with his most devastating secret. He told her he was HIV positive. He had known he had the virus that causes AIDS for a few months but kept it a secret from even his closest friend, his sister. He pleaded with her not to tell their mom and dad until he was ready to tell them. For the next couple of years, as Dave remained relatively healthy, they kept the secret between the two of them. But one Thanksgiving when Dave was home and his health had begun to deteriorate, Diane pleaded with him to tell their parents. His mother had noticed how thin he was getting and was worried about how he was living alone and probably not eating right. But Dave sat down with his mom and dad, and with his sister Diane at his side, he told them the truth.

"They really took it amazingly well," Diane said. For the next three years, Diane spent as much time as she could with her brother. He moved back home as his parents were also extremely compassionate and supportive.

Dave died just before dawn on March 20, 1989. Diane was with him, holding his hand throughout the night. "He squeezed my hand one last time," she said, "and then he died."

A couple of days after Dave's funeral, Diane drove out into the country to their grandparents' farm. Somewhere at the far edge of the property, there was a pond that was hidden by bushes and trees. "It was our favorite spot when we visited Grandma," Diane remembered with a smile. "We used to go skinny-dipping there." She told me how she just sat there at the pond staring at the water, with the cool, early spring breeze brushing her hair and breathing on this gaping wound on her soul.

"So I know why you went to your brother's place after he died," she told me. "You went there not just to remember your brother; you went there to find your future. That's why I went to that pond on my grandma's farm. Because I was afraid to hope that life could go on after Dave died. And somehow, just sitting there in that place that meant so much to us when we were our dad's little scoundrels put me in touch with hope again. I can't explain it, but sitting there, I just knew that life would go on. And even though Dave's absence from my life would never be filled, this wound caused by his death would never quite be healed, I found the courage to go on."

Diane is now married. She and her husband have a son they named Dave. And still, whenever the loss of her brother rises to reveal the emptiness in her heart caused by his death, she goes to that pond on her grandma's farm for awhile and allows the breezes over the pond, and the gentle breath of the Spirit, to fill her with the presence of her brother. It is a presence, real and eternal, that gives her the hope she needs to carry on.

The Fourth Watch of the Night

After Dave's death, Diane went to a place she had known before, a place where memories of love linger on the landscape. This is the same place where Elijah went: to God's holy mountain so steeped in sacred memories. It is also the place Jesus went before he walked on the water and met the disciples in their fear. It is the place we can go to when compassion runs thin, and doubts crowd in and despair pins hope on the mat, winning the best two out of three falls. This is the place we can go to when the work overwhelms us, fatigue at helping others gets the best of us and weariness settles in our souls. We go to that sacred, secluded spot that is absent of people but crowded with memories.

We run — or at least want to run — and hide for awhile and allow whatever it is that is causing us to run away in the first place to stop us in our tracks, to sit us down on the ground of our being and to allow the pain, the fatigue, the doubt and the despair to sink in the soil of our soul. And as the pain goes deeper, we discover that God is not in the storm that splits the mountain or the earthquake that shakes the very foundation of our existence. God is not in the harsh winds that chill us to the bone or the fire that causes all our dreams to go up in smoke and flame. No, God is in the tiny whisper, the gentle breath of a breeze brushing across the water.

Jesus and the disciples' experience in the story about the storm at sea validates this claim that the "tiny, whispering sound" has on our souls. Whereas Mark situates this passage in the context of Jesus wanting to get a breather from ministry after feeding the five thousand, Matthew places this story in the chapter that begins with the death of Jesus' cousin, John the Baptist. We have already reflected on how Jesus, upon hearing of John's death, wanted to steal away some quiet time but the people kept coming after him. We remember how compassion flowed through the cracks of his broken heart and he fed the large crowd with a few loaves of bread. Then, finally, as in Mark's Gospel, Jesus found some time to be alone, in prayer, in silent communion with God.

After soaking in the silence for most of the night, Jesus became aware that the disciples were lost at sea. So he set out toward them. Jesus came to them out of his solitude.

I am struck by the timing of Jesus' stroll across the sea of Galilee in Matthew's Gospel. "It was the fourth watch of the night (Mt. 14: 25)." In navigation circles, the fourth watch of the night is just before dawn. The fourth watch of the night is a good time to pray. It's so very dark just before dawn. And the darkest hour is always the best time to sit in silence.

Diane's brother, Dave, died just before dawn, at the fourth watch of the night. Diane had spent the night with her brother, holding his hand, wiping his brow. Just before he died, he squeezed her hand one more time. Maybe that was the time, just before dawn, at the fourth watch of the night, when Dave saw Jesus walking toward him and inviting him to step out of the boat. Maybe Dave was the most brave when he let go of his sister's hand and took another hand stretched out to him across the water.

Certainly that was Peter's experience when he saw Jesus in the storm. He wanted Jesus to prove it was really him and not a ghost. "Lord, if it is you, bid me come to you on the water (Mt. 14: 28)." Jesus invited him to step out of the boat. Peter responded, but as he got closer to Jesus, he began to sink. His initial faith in stepping out on the water was fragile against the strong winds of fear. This is not unusual. The story underscores how fear often gets the best of us the closer we get to the Divine Presence in our lives. We start off with great courage and zeal and believe nothing can stop us. But the longer we are out on the water, the more the waves of indifference or frustration and the winds of rage or opposition blow against us. Our initial risk is lost in self-doubt. Can I really do this? What am I doing out here? Why in the world did I ever step out of the boat? And so we begin to sink, soaked with self-pity and drenched by fear.

The closer we get to the Divine Mystery, the more awesome the reality becomes. Elijah hid his face in his cloak. Peter began to sink. But "Jesus immediately reached out his hand and caught him (Mt. 14: 31)."

In our lives, when we are lost at sea and it is the fourth watch of the night, for healing to happen we must allow Jesus to walk toward us. And when Jesus comes out of solitude and walks on the water, he brings the dawn. The dawn of hope. "Do not be afraid," Jesus tells us again. "Do not be afraid to hope."

There are times in life when we must run away from the problems and pain. Yet we can run in full retreat, not as an escape, but in response to an invitation to find some solid, sacred ground on which to stand. There, surrounded by the sound of sheer silence, we will find a courage we never knew we had to not only face our problems but to get through them. This is what solitude teaches us; it encourages us to get under our problems, not over them. When we go deeper and sink into the sound of sheer silence, we find the Divine Presence that dares us to hope again.

Whatever it might be that is causing us to be on the run, know that when we run to the solitude of a familiar place, we have come to a good space. In our solitude, we may not find an answer to our problem or a remedy for our pain, but we will find a presence that will remind us we are not alone. For here, walking across the turbulent waters of our fears and tears, there is a tiny whispering sound that reminds us: "Take heart, it is I; do not be afraid" (Mt. 14: 27).

When we take this invitation to our own broken heart, we will not be afraid to hope. We will find the courage to carry on.

In the Eye of the Storm

Paradigms for the Conspiracy

We move backwards in the direction of solitude, silence and prayer not only to feel our own personal pain and loss more deeply, but to feel the pain of the world more intensely. It may seem strange that the first step we must take to become a compassionate presence in our world is backwards, but solitude is the best place to begin this conspiracy.

With so much destruction in the world, it seems paradoxical that solitude would be such an important part of the paradigm for our breathing together in this conspiracy of compassion. A reason why solitude is so central is found in a Bill Moyers' interview on public television I heard several years ago. Since I caught the program in the middle of the conversation, I don't recall the name of the person with whom Moyers was speaking, but Moyers was asking him about his experiences in World War II. He asked him how he maintained a sense of hope in the midst of the violence and death that swirled around him.

The person related an experience that happened to him long after the war. He and his family were caught in a hurricane near their home on the east coast. The hurricane was whirling about them, uprooting trees, destroying homes and leaving havoc and devastation in its wake. But at one point during the storm, he saw the eye of the hurricane and discovered, to his surprise, a patch of blue sky.

Within each of us, he said, there are spaces that are good and holy and peaceful. Our challenge is to enlarge those patches of blue even as the evil whirls around us. This is how he survived the horror of war: by going within himself and tending to that sacred space of hope that is within every human heart.

In our prayer and solitude, we seek to enlarge those spaces and places of hope within us by allowing God's voice to stretch our hearts, our minds and our imaginations. When we retreat to solitude and silence, God's Spirit, like a gentle breeze on a summer morning, stirs within to make us aware of the possibility of compassion. By parenting this possibility in prayer, we expand those patches of promise within us while offering the hospitality of hope to many in our world who feel the hurricane-like forces of war, oppression and injustice.

The place to begin to foster a sense of peace in our own souls and peace in our world is the realm of solitude. In solitude we tend to the patch of blue sky that is the eye of the storm.

Active Resistance

The Desert Fathers and Mothers of ancient Egypt understood this paradigm. To explain why they retreated to the wilderness rather than rolling up their sleeves and getting actively involved in the concerns of the world, they often used the image of seeing the world as a sea filled with the wreckage of humanity. They knew they would be of little value if they simply swam out to try to save the folks who were drowning in despair. If they only treaded water in these raging seas of discontent fueled by ferocious storms of hatred, they would surely drown. Instead, they chose to find some firm ground in prayer and silence.

Yet their stance in the desert was not a passive resignation to the forces of evil but an active resistance to these forces bent on the destruction of human dignity and dreams. Perhaps as ancient hurricane watchers tracking the storms of their day, they knew hurricanes lose much of their power when they come ashore. In the friction between the violent winds of the hurricane and the rugged terrain of the ground on which they stood, the storm would begin to lose much of its energy. Though they were realistic enough to know that heavy rains may continue for awhile, once the hurricane arrives on land the air pressure rises and the winds begin to die down. By firmly planting their feet on the solid ground of solitude, the Desert Fathers and Mothers felt they could create some sacred space where others in the world might find a measure of safety amid the storms of life.

In our own desire for solitude, we seek to create a space for peace within our hearts. As the storms of the world continue to increase in their velocity, we retreat to solitude not to escape the problems of the world but rather to allow God to enlarge that patch of promise and peace within our hearts.

This is how solitude leads to solidarity. We seek solitude to learn from God how to best utilize our gifts of compassion. When we retreat to solitude, we hold the world in our heart, not at arm's length. Certainly someone like Thomas Merton, who lived as a Trappist and spent the last few years of his life in a hermitage, is remembered as a champion of social justice, a maker of peace and a prophet for the inclusive nature of God not because he walked the picket line or demonstrated at nuclear weapons facilities or put his life on the line in active witness against the war in Vietnam. He is remembered as a prophet for peace precisely because he lived a life of solitude and saw his silence as the eye of the hurricane. "In solitude," Merton wrote, "in the depths of one's aloneness, lie the resources for resistance to injustice."

In the silence, we trace those attitudes within us that cause our hearts to shrink. In solitude, we come face to face with our fears. In solitude, we scrape beneath the surface — the superficial image of who we are in the eyes of the world or even the eyes of our friends — and are caught in the gaze of God. It is God's eye that surveys this heartland of ours in solitude. God's eye stares at us and makes us uncomfortable. But the longer God stares, the more compelled we are to go within to see if we can observe what God has perceived. In the eye of the storm, in solitude, God's eye directs our view not only to our fears and flaws, but more essentially to our gifts and dreams — those resources that lie deep within us — to offer resistance to injury and injustice.

Solitude teaches us mindfulness — expanding our minds to their full capacity in order to include even those with whom we disagree. In the eye of the storm, prayer becomes the spiritual exercise that stretches our heart in order to hold even those we find most difficult to love.

Resting in the gaze of God, we humbly admit our need for Divine intervention. We embrace what it means to be human: made in God's image yet vulnerable, fragile and fearful. In this solitary space in the eye of the storm, our vulnerability exposes who we are; we hold nothing back. This allows God to give us a new perspective which will help us to discover our dreams — those gifts we have received from God that nurture hope within us and widen our inner space of peace.

Hurricane Annie

Such a solitary and visionary quest is never easy nor convenient. It may even make others suspicious as they wonder why we have become such "private eyes." But that is precisely what we are doing when we go into solitude: Like a private eye we search for the clues God has hidden in our own experiences that will help us find the way of compassion. That is what a woman called "Hurricane Annie" discovered when she went looking for the eye amid the storms of her life.

Annie's life was a whirlwind of activity. As a lawyer, she was a public defender who labored tirelessly for justice for the poor, spending countless hours interviewing clients and preparing cases. As a friend, she was a private defender of the value of deep and lasting relationships that had to be nurtured with creativity and care if they were to survive. But one day, after losing a case for a client she cared about deeply and losing a friend she had known for years, Annie realized she needed some space. Her losses had accumulated like so many dark clouds, and now the skies had opened and too many tears had saturated her world with a great sadness. Though she was fond of that nickname her friends had given her because of her lifestyle, she had always thought she was the "eye" for others in the storms of their lives. But now she had lost her eye, her center. It was time to retreat.

So Annie went to a secret place with no forwarding address. Solitude would be her only companion. She believed that only by being silent could she listen for the divine dream taking shape in her soul. She spent her days contemplating the wind rustling in the trees. Her eyes open, she watched and listened. She listened with her eyes. What she heard confirmed that there was a symmetry, even a synergy, and an energy force that formed around her, that came from within her. Then she knew: The healing of her own wounds, of the earth, of the universe, comes from within the heart and soul of the contemplative. Here she gathered all the scattered and shattered pieces of God's dream for the world into her own fragile body. She held them all without expectation. She raised them to the Divine Dreamer without petition or the promise of an answer. Annie grew weary lifting all the heaviness of her losses and the losses experienced by humanity — the weight of bewilderment, the tons of tears, the pounds of pride and prejudice. In her silence, this much came into focus: Annie knew that deep compassion and true peace could come only when she allowed God to create enough room in her heart to hold even the sharp edges of her own broken dreams, jagged and cruel.

At one point in her sacred sojourn, Annie realized that the search for Shalom, for true peace, is never about the absence of war — whether that war is waged in one's heartland or in a place known as the holy land — but about the presence of God. So to seek Shalom is to seek God. But this elusive quest is fruitless unless one first concludes that God is too large to be found. The seeker must be content to be found by the Divine Presence, not the other way around.

In solitude, God intrudes, surprises, startles. The contemplative causes nothing. Nothingness is the goal of solitude so one can be filled with the "somethingness" of God. Here is something: "You are mine," God says. "You belong to me." Here is something else: "Live on in my love." And something more: "Peace I give to you." Searching for peace is destiny deferred; one cannot chase a gift. One must be humble enough to receive a gift.

But once received, the gift must be given away without condition or cause. Seekers of solitude who keep the peace only for themselves lose the gift. The contemplative, though hidden from the world's view, is intricately connected to the world. Separation from others is for the sake of being found by Shalom. And once found, the compassionate contemplative must then live in the world in such a way that others sense a stirring of deeper truth, a longing for that something else that so far has remained unsatisfied. The solitary person must yearn to be connected with community.

Compassionate people move back and forth, in and out, between silence and story. They move gracefully — full of the grace given in solitude — into their world, giving as a gift the gift they have been given. Awakening the world to a deeper truth, they startle and intrude in much the same way the divine dream shook them. And if they go away again, out of sight but never far from mind, they go with the intent that the world is not healed yet because they are not healed. They go to be found again by the dream, and this movement continues until all is one with the Divine Dreamer.

Our quest for solitude nurtures creativity in us. In the eye of the storm we look out upon our world from our prayerful hearts and begin to sense that the answer to our prayer is not in *doing* more but *being* more. Then, when we gather with those with whom we pray on a regular basis, we seek to create an atmosphere of trust where we allow stories of our own solitary experiences to spill out upon the floor. We reverence these tales of woe and wonder, and we realize there is very little we can *do* except *be* present to each other.

Yet in listening to these stories and reverencing these moments of self-revelation, we can also begin to piece together ways to respond to the suffering we see but so often feel impotent to impact with our lives. In our contemplative listening to the story of another, we begin to sense the wisdom of the Sufi teaching: "When the power of love overcomes the love of power, there will be true peace." The power of this love, a power generated in silence by the awesome gaze of divine love, teaches us how powerless we are to solve the problems of another. But in our listening to the other with contemplative eyes, we have already moved into compassionate action. The other has found a safe place in which to tell her story.

When "Hurricane Annie" returned to her work as a public defender, her clients noticed something different about her. "You seem to listen with your eyes more than your ears," one said to her. "Most people are busy taking notes and thinking about their next case, but you pay attention to me and my story." And when her friends welcomed her back from her Sabbath time, they also noticed her eyes. "Annie," they said, "your eyes hold a certain calmness now. They seem a deeper blue. Are you wearing new contacts?"

No, Annie wasn't wearing new contacts, but she was in contact, in touch, with a deeper truth during her solitude time. And now she brought a glimpse of Shalom, a glance of grace, a vision of integrity and of wholeness she discovered in solitude, to the community of her work and the company of her friends. Being caught in the gaze of the divine eye and "praying attention" to the divine dream in her silence, Annie was better able to pay attention to all sides of another's story.

Coming to Compassionate Faith

A Scripture story which reflects this process of how a "private eye" is opened to a larger vision of faith and community is found in John's Gospel (Jn. 9: 1-41). This fascinating tale about the man born blind offers a second paradigm for the formation of communities of compassion. By tracing the faith development of the man born blind, we see how our own coming to compassionate faith follows a similar track. We discover that an essential dimension of communities of compassion is the art of storytelling. If we are to conspire together, we must trust the truth of our own stories and be willing to tell our faith stories to others. We must be open enough to hold another's story with great reverence. And in such uncommon sharing of our stories we find the eye of the hurricane growing larger as the storms surrounding us begin to dissipate.

First, recall the story from John's Gospel. Jesus and his disciples have come upon a man who has never seen the light of day. He has lived his whole life in the darkness, being blind from birth. The question the disciples pose about whose fault it was that this man was born blind misses the point. What is important is that the light has come to extinguish the darkness. With the presence of Jesus, dawn hovers on the horizon. Sight is about to return.

Jesus spits on the ground, makes a mud pie (perhaps like he used to do in Nazareth when he was growing up), places the mud pack on the man's eyes and tells him to go take a "bath." When he returns, the man can see.

But here the story takes an interesting turn that changes it from a simple story about a miracle to a profound parable about coming to the quality of faith necessary to live in the reign of God, the foundational faith upon which our conspiracy of compassion is constructed. The man can see images and appearances, but he cannot yet see with the inner eye of faith. As the story unfolds, we see how the man comes to faith. We witness the process of faith development.

First, he is confronted by his neighbors, who recognize him as the young man who begged for a living. When they ask him what happened, he tells them that the "man called Jesus" cured him. Jesus is still simply a man who has an extraordinary talent for healing. The young man who has been cured is not yet on the threshold of discipleship because he did not follow Jesus after being healed. This conversation with his neighbors is the first opportunity for the man to share his faith. That faith was still in its infancy, based on an encounter with a man named Jesus. A remarkable encounter to be sure: The man has been physically healed and is able to see his mother and father and friends for the first time in his life. But a spiritual healing has not yet occurred. It is reasonable to assume that the man could have stayed at this level for the rest of his life. As it happens, the next step to faith is quickly unfolding. His neighbors, so confused by this whole episode, take him to the religious leaders for their opinion about the matter.

The Pharisees show themselves as people more interested in the means than the end. They are less concerned about a man's sight being restored than they are about the technicalities of how he was healed. They are more interested in the method than the message. After all, it is the Sabbath, and making mud pies on the Sabbath is against the law. They interrogate the man born blind, and he tells the story again. But on this second telling, the vision of faith starts coming more into focus. Like having our eyes dilated and then living with blurred vision for a few hours until it returns to normal, the man's image of Jesus is becoming clearer. As the Pharisees debate about Jesus' identity, they finally ask the man who had been cured what he thinks, and the man with a now 20/40 faith vision replies, "He is a prophet."

Being skeptical scholars, the Pharisees call in the man's parents to verify that he had been blind from birth. His parents, not wanting to get involved, state the obvious: "Yes, this is our son and he was blind at birth. But we have no idea how or why he can see now. Let him speak for himself." Though the parents were thrilled that their son can now see, they don't want to get into a controversy. After all, they have probably not as yet unpacked their suitcases of the guilt and shame at their son having been born blind. They carry with them the baggage that they must have done something terribly wrong to deserve such a fate as a blind son. Now that he is healed, their guilt is replaced by fear. If they acknowledge Jesus as the Messiah, they will be expelled from the synagogue.

Once again the man born blind is called in to testify. By this time he is a little testy because he's told the story so many times. Repetition may seem mundane, but the value in telling the story over and over again becomes clear. Now the man's faith vision is 20/30 because in this telling he defends this prophet who opened his eyes: "You do not know where he comes from, and yet he opened my eyes. We know that God does not listen to sinners, but if anyone is a worshiper of God and does God's will, God listens to that one."

The man has reached the point in his faith development to see that Jesus must come from God, that he is not a fraud looking for fame and fortune but is devout and follows the will of God. This man has indeed has come a long way, but there is still some way to go before his vision is 20/20.

Questioned further, he says, "Never since the world began has it been heard that anyone opened the eyes of a person born blind. If this man were not from God, he could do nothing." Now the man is finally able to read the tiny letters on the bottom of the chart. He articulates what he was alluding to earlier and bluntly proclaims his belief that Jesus must be from God.

For this newly-found faith, the man is promptly thrown out of the temple.

The final checkpoint on this journey of coming to faith occurs when Jesus hears of the man's expulsion from the temple and seeks him out. Remarkable, isn't it, that it is not the man who went looking for Jesus but the other way around. Even though the formerly blind man is not looking (indicating that everything is still a bit fuzzy), he is found by Jesus.

"Do you believe in the Son of Man?" Jesus asks him.

"And who is he, sir, that I may believe in him?"

"You have seen him," Jesus replies. "It is he who speaks to you."

"Lord, I believe," the man says, bowing down to worship him.

He has come full circle in his journey of faith; the healing, both physical and spiritual, is now complete. The ritual question that Jesus asks him — "Do you believe?" — is extremely important for firmly grounding a 20/20 faith vision; just as the words of commitment in all of the sacraments underscore the meaning of the sacraments. By articulating his belief in Jesus, the man born blind has become a disciple of Christ who no longer lives in darkness but now walks in the light of the Lord.

The story says that our conversion in the ways of compassion takes time. It reminds us that for most of us conversion is not an instantaneous occurrence but an ongoing discovery. We are always in process, and one of the primary components in this process is the willingness to share our faith with others.

The risks of such storytelling are apparent: The authorities will question us; few will believe us; even our families might leave us on our own because of their own fear of getting involved. But when we find those who are willing to listen and who challenge us to articulate what we believe, we will come to know the power and truth of our own stories. These are the people with whom we will cultivate the courage necessary to hurry the dawn.

A Community of Healers

One such personal experience in 1985 suggests a third paradigm for how to participate in this conspiracy of compassion. But before I tell the story, I want to share a metaphor that puts the experience in context for me.

At St. Mary's Grade School in the suburbs of St. Louis, we played a game called "Across the Line." In those days (the late 1960s), a white line was drawn across the asphalt of the playground. The meaning was clear: Boys played on one side, girls on the other. One of the sisters monitored the line, armed with a bell to signal the end of recess or sometimes the crime of a trespasser.

Across the Line was not an original game. It was a variation of the ancient ritual of "Keep Away." The object was simple: The boy with the ball would try to elude his opponents and attempt to reach the promised land across the line. No tackling was allowed (the sisters frowned on the rough stuff), but still the game produced its share of skinned knees, torn trousers and bruised egos.

I thought of that childhood game on Valentine's Day in 1985 when I crossed another line. This white line was not painted on a playground but on serious ground. Deadly serious ground. It was the demarcation line at the Strategic Air Command based outside of Omaha. I was there with more than 400 others to sing, to pray and to celebrate a liturgy of resistance. In the cold wind, locked arm in arm, we sang songs of peace and prayed to a God of life. We celebrated our solidarity with all the victims, real and potential, of the nuclear arms race.

This liturgy of protest climaxed a three-day retreat on nonviolence that was hosted by Bishop Maurice Dingman of Des Moines. He invited us to reflect on the power of nonviolent resistance to stop the maddening race toward "mutual assured destruction." Bishop Dingman called for the retreat as a response to the 1983 United States Catholic Bishops' pastoral, *The Challenge of Peace*. In that document, he and his companion bishops challenged North American Catholics to move from discussion and reflection about peace to witness and action.

The spiritual guides on this journey of resistance included Jim Wallis of Sojourners, Mary Evelyn Jegen of Pax Christi and Fr. Dan Berrigan. Wallis quoted a recent statement by a general who told a group of military personnel that "the greatest challenge to all we do today comes from the churches." He reminded the retreatants that the author of our resistance to evil in the world is Jesus. "Jesus was killed," he said, "because he was a threat to the ruling authorities."

To the tune of the civil rights anthem "We Shall Overcome," the men, women and children gathered in prayer and sang "We Are Not Afraid." As Wallis cautioned the group, "We need more than resistance; we need hope. And the surest sign of hope is the Resurrection. The only thing that can kill hope now is if we forget the Resurrection."

Resurrection was the theme of these days as we listened and prayed to the Spirit of life and love for guidance and courage. "The Resurrection was a crime," Berrigan said. "The dead are supposed to remain dead! Just as the execution of Christ was perfectly legal, so the Resurrection was manifestly illegal. Even Pilate posted a guard at the tomb, the message being, 'Stay in there!'"

Berrigan's words fueled the fires of indecision that raged inside. I had come to the retreat almost certain that I would not cross the line at SAC. I had never committed civil disobedience before, and as I wrote my provincial before the retreat asking him for his prayers, I said I probably would not get arrested unless the Spirit really did a number on me during the retreat. Well, the tongues of fire were not visible over our heads, but they were obvious in the hearts of the participants and flowed from the mouths of the speakers. "Christianity began with an illegal act by Christ," Berrigan noted, "and so criminalized his followers."

It was not without cause that Berrigan used as his point of departure the story of Pentecost in the Acts of the Apostles. Huddled in fear and blinded by the loss of Jesus, the disciples were given the gift of the Spirit and so left the upper room to face a waiting, wounded world. They became healers in that broken world — grace-filled ministers of peace who touched the blind and made them see, who invited the lame to get up and dance, who encouraged the frustrated with words of hope. "Pentecost created a community of healers," Berrigan said.

Those were the words that whirled inside me as I wrestled with the choice that loomed before me: to cross or not to cross the line. As the journey of resistance to the SAC base began, I also thought of the words of Jesus: "Do this in memory of me." In the end, I felt the choice was the same that confronts all people of faith: life or death. One step, backward or forward, held enormous consequence for me. A step backward meant safety and security. A step forward meant risk and growth. A step backward meant compromise. A step forward meant commitment.

On that Valentine's Day, the feast of love and friendship, we gathered one more time for prayer and to be sent forth to meet the forces of death. When we sang "Here I am, Lord," the words took on new meaning and new power. When we sang "Be Not Afraid," I felt the burden of fear being lifted from my heart. At the ritual immediately before leaving for the SAC base, when my hands were anointed with oil, my choice had been sealed.

Standing on the safe side of the line that Valentine's Day, I thought of Isaiah's prayer: "Make firm the knees that are weak." And words Mary Evelyn Jegen spoke the day before echoed in my mind as I looked across the line at the soldiers in green fatigues: "Do I love the men and women inside the SAC base? Can I go there with enough love and care and compassion to start a dialogue?"

That conversation began with a statement read by Bishop Dingman. The songs were sung, and in the distance a drumbeat for peace filled the open air. (Ironically, the man beating the drum was arrested a few hours later for the crime of "disturbing the peace.") Then, in groups of 15 or 20, we crossed the line and knelt down. There was not a teacher to ring the bell of alarm, but a sergeant who ordered us to disperse. There were no skinned knees or torn trousers or bruised egos. But like that game we used to play at St. Mary's, I knew the consequences for crossing the line.

As I was escorted to the bus, searched and driven to the place of detention, my conscience was clear. For those few hours of confinement, as my picture was taken and my fingerprints etched on a card, there had been no compromise, no stepping back, no second thoughts. For those few hours, I was free.

There are many lines drawn on the landscape of our lives. There are boundaries that become barriers to intimacy, community, solidarity. That faith and resistance retreat led me to cross inner, personal lines as well as outward, cultural lines. It was truly a conspiracy of compassion. As we conspired for justice and peace, I felt the Spirit breathing new life into my tired and trembling bones, opening my heart a little more to embrace the wounds of a heavy world.

Children of Light

Violent storms of injustice, oppression and war continue to rage in our world creating so much darkness. St. Paul in his letter to the Ephesians alludes to how deep this darkness can be: "Once you were darkness, but now you are light in the Lord; walk as children of light" (Eph. 5: 8). Notice how Paul does not say that we lived *in* darkness but we *were* darkness. When one lives in darkness one can blame other forces that created the dark. But when one is identified with the darkness, there is no one else to blame. The night has taken over. We live and move and have our being in the dark. We are night stalkers rather than day trippers.

When this is the case, it is not so easy to turn on the light. When we have become one with the darkness, this intimacy of mind and body and soul with night will conceive deeds of darkness. It's in our genes. Ambassadors of evil. Children of the night.

But this is part of the process of our conspiracy. We must not take the darkness for granted. We must have the courage to acknowledge its existence not only in the world but in ourselves. Admitting this, we come to see how Jesus is the light that walks in the night of our sin and turns the night into day.

As people engaged in a conspiracy of compassion, we hear the alarm clock ringing in the darkness of our days. Instead of hitting the snooze alarm, rolling over, hiding under the covers and stealing a few more minutes of sleep, we are roused from our deathlike sleep to greet the dawn of compassion in our day. To live as children of light so that even if there is deep darkness around us, even if we are surrounded by dense fog, it does not seep inside us.

By focusing our attention on the one who wakes us and shakes us from our sleep, we become lighthouses that serve as beacons of hope for those lost in the fog of despair.

This was brought home to me many years ago when I participated in another event that has become for me a paradigm of this conspiracy of compassion, a beacon in imagining ways in which our breathing together through our wounds can turn the darkness into day. That night several years ago, I met a young girl named Karla. She was four years old then, and her eyes told a thousand stories. On this night, however, they were fighting back sleep, not tears. She and her family had just arrived at the cathedral in Davenport, Iowa, and were welcomed by 200 singing, applauding supporters.

Karla's mother and father, Jose and Marina, and her brother and sister, Juan and Claudia, had just completed a long and perilous journey to accept sanctuary in Davenport. For more than three years they had been on the run, depending on the generosity and hospitality of strangers. Like the disciples who were sent by Jesus to proclaim the reign of God, Jose, Marina and their children were also proclaiming a reign — a reign of terror.

I could not tell if they were smiling that night when they walked into the cathedral because red bandannas covered their faces. They were protecting their own anonymity, but even more they were concerned for their relatives and friends in El Salvador who might have to bear the consequences of their flight to sanctuary. I could not see their smiles, but I could see their eyes. They were weary and exhausted but now safe in the company of strangers.

The family had left El Salvador in March, 1981, under a threat of death. Jose, who worked in a government position and was active in a labor union, was expecting the worst after two of his coworkers and their families were murdered. So he and his wife gathered their two children and fled into the night.

At the cathedral that night, Jose told his story through an interpreter. It was a tale of late-night escapes and close brushes with death, of living for eight months in the shell of a house under construction where they endured flies, mosquitoes, cockroaches and rats. He told of slipping past border guards by slipping them some money and running for almost three hours in the early morning. "Those were the longest three hours of my life," Jose said.

But this was also a story of hope and of life. For on the way, Marina gave birth to their first son. By the time they arrived in Iowa, Juan was two years old. The photographers could not get enough pictures of him and his two sisters as their clicking cameras punctuated Jose's story of pain and promise. "We are here," Jose said, "trying to save the most precious gift that God has given us — our lives."

That night in Davenport, Jose, Marina, Karla, Claudia and Juan gave that precious gift of life as gift to those who offered them a home and a safe harbor from their years of exile. Those who welcomed them took a grave risk as well since they were challenging the law that labelled this family *economic* rather than *political* refugees. But then, as someone once said, "Compassion obscures the consequences of an action." In the exchange of stories, strangers became friends. Hearts were moved as the reign of God eclipsed the reign of fear.

When we are motivated by compassion for another, then the risks become small, unable to be measured. We act only out of need, the need to love and be loved. Such love, as it shined in the eyes of a four-year-old girl named Karla, is the only motivation most of us ever need to be compassionate.

God's image is seen so clearly in the tears of a father in Sarajevo holding his dead son, in the eyes of a frightened child seeking sanctuary, in the face of a tired young mother in a soup kitchen line, in the calloused hands of a farmer and factory worker, in the haunting glance of one who dies alone. But we become so accustomed to the sights of suffering that we often fail to notice.

It takes courage to raise our voices even when the world is still in the dark. It takes courage for us to touch the fears and wipe the tears of those we meet along the way. But we find the courage to do so when we breathe deeply God's unconditional fidelity and love for us. This gives us the courage to act on our convictions. This gives us the permission to raise our voices against evil.

God's Spirit anoints us to bring glad tidings to the poor by standing in solidarity with them, not keeping them at arm's length but embracing them with a compassion born of the cross.

God's Breath beckons us to bring liberty to captives by unlocking the doors slammed shut by greed, using the keys of generosity, charity and, most of all, justice. It calls us to release those imprisoned by the bottom line of corporate profits, which see only statistics and miss the sacredness of the individual.

God's Wind carries us to bring recovery of sight to those blinded by materialism — those whose eyes have been closed by the notion that every want is a need; those who see only possessions and lose sight of the dignity of the human person.

God's Spirit nurtures courage in us to raise our voices above the din of the crowd, to show a new way to those whose lives are imprisoned by militarism; courage to point out to those who see only dollar signs, the signs that lead to the reign of God — meekness, humility, mercy and righteousness; courage to model reconciliation for those whose energies are fueled by revenge.

In the hurricane-like forces of evil that seek to destroy the dignity and dreams of human beings, God is the eye of the storm. Our participation in this conspiracy of compassion places us directly in God's eye. With God's grace, and under God's gracious gaze, we seek to make this eye so large that the forces of evil lose their strength now and forever.

Second Wind

The Pentecost Conspiracy

As we seek to enlarge the eye of the storm by forming communities of compassion, our basic text for this conspiracy is the second chapter of the Acts of the Apostles. Here we read how the first followers of Jesus, inspired by his Spirit, embraced the challenge of their founder and servant leader after his resurrection and ascension into heaven. In tracking the wind currents that sweep through this passage from Acts, we feel the power and sense the promise that this conspiracy of compassion holds for our day.

As they were walking to the house where they would meet, everything was calm. It was so still that even the leaves resisted the invitation to dance. Someone remarked at how quiet it seemed. "Perhaps it is the calm before the storm," another said.

How true that was. A few minutes after the last person had arrived — Thomas, I think it was — they heard a sound "like the rush of a mighty wind, and it filled all the house where they were sitting" (Acts 2: 2). One can safely assume they were not sitting for long.

I have never been in a tornado, but I have heard people describe the sound: "It was like a train roaring through the house." Tornadoes, of course, are destructive and sometimes deadly. But the funnel cloud of fury that enveloped the house where the disciples were staying was fueled by the Holy Spirit. The only thing that wind destroyed was fear. For this was a life-giving blast that swept away caution even as courage swelled in the disciples' souls.

With their hair and clothes blowing wildly in the wind, they grabbed onto chairs, tables and each other and held on for dear life. After all, that was the point the Spirit was making: life. Strangely enough, they were not afraid. They were not blown away. They remained as calm as the air before the storm. And even when the Spirit dangled flames of fire over their heads, which shot like lasers into their stomachs, dissolving the knots there, they were not afraid. Their doubt had now been transformed into hope, their fear into fire. The oppressive dread that had knocked the wind out of them was gone. They could breathe freely again.

They were filled with the Breath of the Holy Spirit and they began to speak as the Spirit prompted them. But the Spirit was not a ventriloquist who put words into their mouths. No, the Spirit was now giving them new languages to speak the words of love to all the world. They had become new women and men — nothing could stop them now! They were a Pentecost people! The conspiracy was on! The conspiracy of compassion that would change the world.

Those who heard these strange sounds coming from the house were amazed. Some were envious: "Sounds like a great party!" Others were enraged: "They are all drunk!" Both were right. They did have too much wine — the new wine of compassion. Not the wine that would make their minds fuzzy, their legs stagger, their bodies fall. This new wine cleared their minds, strengthened their weak knees and pulsed through their bodies with Pentecost passion. This was a party of divine inspiration, a party of divine invitation where the guest list was as long as God's right arm. In other words, everyone was invited!

A New Creation Community

The effects of the Spirit rushing through that house where the first disciples had gathered are astonishing. At the end of the second chapter of Acts we learn:

They devoted themselves to the apostles' instruction and to the communal life, to the breaking of the bread and the prayers. A reverent fear overtook them all, for many wonders and signs were performed by the apostles. Those who believed shared all things in common; they would sell their property and goods, dividing everything on the basis of each one's need. They went to the temple area together every day, while in their homes they broke bread. With exultant and sincere hearts they took their meals in common, praising God and winning the approval of all the people (Acts 2: 42-47).

This passage contains four basic breathing exercises for creating what we might call new creation communities that reflect the conspiracy of compassion: Tell the story, reverence the tradition, respond to the needs and break the bread. But before we can practice these breathing lessons, we should first acknowledge that when we read this passage, we sometimes brush it off as idealistic and not attainable. We dismiss this ideal because we so often miss the first prerequisite for living in a way that allows us to breathe upon each others' wounds as those first disciples did. As we outlined in the very beginning, we must first develop the gift to read our own wounds in a way that enables us to trace the wounds on the body of Christ.

Reading wounds is not an easy exercise. It makes us uncomfortable. It certainly isn't something we do in polite company. But our wounds are required reading for anyone who seeks to live in the Spirit of the risen Christ. Otherwise, the story from the Acts of the Apostles which outlines the side effects that the breath of the nail-scarred Lord had on his first followers will seem too idealistic to ever be real.

Remember how before the breath of the Holy Spirit swept away their fears in that windblown house these first disciples had already caught their breath by inhaling the promise of Jesus when he said, "Peace be with you," breathing on them in the upper room after the crucifixion. The members of the early Christian community could not have lived in the way the Acts of the Apostles describes unless they had allowed the breath of Jesus in that upper room to blow gently into their wounded hopes, their damaged dreams, their scarred souls. But when Jesus breathed upon those fearful folk crowded in the cramped space of that upper room — that place where there was no breathing room because all the doors were locked and windows shut — this first breath of a new creation filled their lungs, their hearts, their hopes again.

When this first fresh breath of the Risen One is followed by the rush of the Spirit Wind in the story from Acts, we see what a difference these two very different currents — a breath-like whisper and a howling wind — made in their lives! They had had a chance to conspire, to breathe together into their wounds during the time they waited in the upper room after Jesus had ascended. Now that the Spirit Wind had breathed on them, they dedicated themselves to living this Pentecost conspiracy. They cultivated a quality of community life marked by listening to each one's stories, praying with each one's hurts, responding to each one's need and breaking bread in each one's company.

A wondrous spring breeze swept across the parched, dry heartland of those first followers of Jesus. It created a community the world has not seen since but may someday see again if only we are open to "receiving the Holy Spirit." This "receiving" involves our inhaling the transforming Spirit of life and love, forgiveness and favor, and exhaling whispers of reconciliation and hope upon the wounded hearts of those too fearful, too busy or too broken to believe. If we think this is too idealistic or unattainable, recall something that the famous anthropologist, Margaret Mead, once said: "Never doubt that a group of thoughtful, committed citizens can change the world; indeed, it is the only thing that ever has."

The first breathing exercise that fashioned the first disciples into a new creating community was to tell the story. They "devoted themselves to the apostles' instruction and the communal life." I can't imagine that this "instruction" was focused on doctrine and dogma but rather on the dreams the rabbi shared about the reign of God with those faithful few who followed him along the way. What stories they must have told of all the miracles they witnessed and the misunderstandings they experienced. Stories of how often they missed the point or misinterpreted the meaning of the Messiah's life and death. Recollections of how many disputes arose among them and how many disagreements entangled them even as the rabbi reminded them again and again, "It cannot be that way with you."

The apostles learned from these mistakes. They learned to walk from their missteps that caused them to stumble and fall. They learned to breathe from their own wounds.

So the first breathing exercise of a new creation community is to tell, to breathe out, the stories again and again — and to breathe in, to read and hear them freshly, as if for the first time. These stories never get old because this Holy Spirit that inspired these stories and shapes our own experiences never gets old. Dogma and doctrine may get old, tired, worn and ragged at the edges, but the stories of the Risen One never get old.

The second breathing exercise is to hold a holy breath, to reverence the tradition. The story from the Acts of the Apostles tells that "they went to the Temple" each day to pray. They reverenced the traditions from which this new way was born. They did not dismiss the old way but held their tradition as sacred. This tension between the old way and the new way had to cause hurt and confusion. Certainly later in the story of the Acts of the Apostles we hear some of the disagreements that arose and the conflicts that developed. But the Spirit of this new creation community fashioned a bond between the old and new. They prayed in such a way that all people of all persuasions found more than a measure of peace in the prayer of the community.

This breathing exercise reminds us to reverence the traditions of those who have gone before us. It challenges us to be inclusive of all peoples. It beckons us to believe that in shared, sacred silence before the awesome mystery of the Divine Presence all will find a home. It is so true, isn't it, that today religious language, images and names for God seek to divide so many in the faith community. But when we gather to pray and enter into sacred stillness, there are no walls, no words to keep us apart.

The third breathing exercise calls us to breathe together, to respond to each one's need. Here is the place where compassion in the new creation community finds its name. It is a compassion that comes from breathing into one's own wounds. "They shared all things in common" — all things, not just their material goods or personal property, but their hopes and dreams, the brokenness and their betrayals. The reconciling Spirit created in them an attitude of deferment — deferring to another's need before fulfilling an individual want.

Now this seems very idealistic in a materialistic world. To capitalistic ears it sounds like communism. In a world, and in a self, where wants and real needs seem always at odds, doing battle, jockeying for position and attention, this breathing exercise seeks to remind us that fulfilling another's *need* is all one might ever *want* in life. Such an attitude of deferment is only possible when we all breathe a common breath.

Finally, we breathe out praise. This fourth breathing exercise is really a celebration of the other three. When we tell the stories, reverence the traditions by praying the hurts, and respond to the needs of others, we break the bread in the company of those who once were strangers but now are called friends. With generous and grace-filled hearts, we breathe out praise and break the bread of friendship which we call Eucharist. And as we do, we tell some more stories and the breathing cycle begins again.

One Man's Second Wind

We see the results of how the early Christian community's practice of breathing from their own wounds created such a stir that others were swept up in its holy wind. Because of the way these women and men lived, because of the way they prayed, because of the way they loved, because of the way they cared, more people became attracted to their way of life.

But if we can't fathom how such a community is possible today, or we can't imagine how a new creation community can exist in institutional structures where rituals of exclusion are practiced and harsh words of excommunication are sometimes heard, then perhaps we can find our second wind in the memories of one man who breathed in the fresh air of God's new birth: Peter.

In Peter's story we see the difference between the experience of *transfiguration* and the experience of *transformation*. On the Holy Mountain where Jesus was transfigured, Peter had experienced a spiritual high. But the transfiguration did not transform him. His transformation occurred later — only after the suffering, death and resurrection of Jesus.

Most of Peter's wounds were self-inflicted: the shame of denial and the pride of not wanting to have his feet washed (both of which occurred long after he experienced the transfiguration of Jesus). We have already noted how often Peter was diagnosed with what seemed to be a terminal illness: foot-in-mouth disease. The most extreme case of this dreaded disorder was the night he followed Jesus at a distance after his arrest in the garden and camped out by the fire in the courtyard. While Jesus was on trial in the courthouse, Peter was called on to testify in the courtyard. Three times he denied even knowing Jesus. Realizing that Jesus' prediction at the Last Supper that Peter would deny him three times had come true, Peter ran out of the courtyard and wept bitterly.

This was the beginning of Peter's rehabilitation which led to his transformation. His betrayal of Jesus left a bitter taste in his mouth. He could have given up completely. But instead, he wept. He tasted his own tears, and those tears watered the seeds of his transformation.

Peter's rehabilitation comes full cycle in the story from John's Gospel when Jesus appeared to Peter and a few of his friends on the beach after his resurrection (Jn. 21: 1-19). This story, sometimes referred to as the Breakfast on the Beach, offers us a powerful example of how our conspiracy challenges us to be a community of memory and hope.

This story had its beginning at the Last Supper when Jesus warned Peter and the other disciples that they would desert him. Peter was indignant, saying that even though the others might leave, he would stay with Jesus to the bitter end. But we know what happened.

The appearance of Jesus to Peter and the others on the beach is a story of how Peter came to know Jesus, how his faith and life was restored by the presence of the risen Jesus. The triple denial he uttered that fateful night, "I do not know the man," was now unraveled by Jesus' asking Peter three times, "Do you love me?" And just as he had denied Jesus three times, now Peter affirmed his love for Jesus three times. After the third question, Peter simply asked Jesus to read his heart: "Lord, you know everything; you know well that I love you" (Jn. 21: 17).

As he affirmed his love for Christ, Peter was sent forth to "feed the flock." This was Peter's call and commission. This is our call and commission as well. The story says that our encounter with the risen Jesus invites us, inspires us and challenges us to go forth and create communities of care and compassion, memory and hope. But with this commission comes a caution: It will not be easy. "When you grow old," Jesus said to Peter, "you will stretch out your hand and another will fasten a belt around you and take you where you do not wish to go" (Jn. 21: 18). Like Jesus, Peter would die a bloody death on the cross. Like the Lord he loved, he would stretch out his hands and be crucified. Earlier, Peter did not want to believe that Jesus would have to suffer and die. Now he was brought face to face with the reality of his own suffering and death. The cross is the cost of compassionate discipleship. As Peter embraced this truth, his rehabilitation became complete. He was transformed.

Suffering: Reading Wounds

Jesus' words to Peter on the beach affirm that at the heart of our identity as compassionate people is the question, "Am I willing to suffer?" Living in North America at the dawn of the twenty-first century in a culture that seeks to escape suffering no matter the cost presents an identity crisis. I have been accustomed to a sanitized, safe and secure life in white, middle-class North America. Though I have been raised with Gospel values, I have also been influenced by values that are so often in conflict with the message of Jesus.

A few years ago, I was helping out in a parish. After Mass one Sunday, a woman came up to me and said, "You must have really suffered greatly in your life." I don't recall the Scripture for that day or what I said in the homily, but her comment struck me because I am a product of the "me generation" and I really never felt I knew what it means to suffer. Sure, I've had my share of heartaches and sorrow. I've seen the face of death more than I care to remember. But compared to the suffering I see at a distance — the suffering of my brothers and sisters in so many parts of our world and within my own city and religious community, I considered my suffering to be small and insignificant.

That's true, except it is impossible to measure one's own suffering. To be compassionate, to participate in the conspiracy, does not mean one has to experience every pain and sorrow this world has to offer. It simply means that we are willing to enter into another's pain as best we can. We hold another's suffering not with judgement but with mercy, not with answers but with affection. The Greek root of the word compassion implies such mercy and affection.

But as we all know from experience, this is not easy or done lightly. Compassion takes true courage and hard work. That is why we need to listen and learn from each other, to reverence each other's stories, to read each other's wounds, to gather the courage to live with compassion.

A good friend of mine once told me that her daughter, Stephanie, who as an infant had spinal meningitis, which rendered her unable to hear, was such a gift and blessing to the family. "She has taught us compassion," the mother said. I knew exactly what she meant. For me, my brother Ed was my primary teacher.

Yet Stephanie also taught me something about compassion. And to symbolically seal that lesson she taught me the name for Jesus in sign language: pointing to the palm of one's hand, pointing to the wound. When Stephanie touched her palm, she spoke and heard the name of Jesus.

As co-conspirators, we are invited to read the wounds of the crucified and risen Christ. Not just to glance at them as we might browse quickly through the headlines in the morning paper, but to study them closely. When Jesus showed his disciples his hands and his side, he was the sign language of love: The resurrected body of Christ is wounded.

The body of Christ still bears the marks of crucifixion. But like the one who was absent the day Jesus appeared to the disciples in the upper room, we fail to see these wounds. And unless we see them, we won't believe the wounds are there.

We have come to call him "Doubting Thomas" in our tradition. But it would be closer to the truth to call him "Disbelieving Thomas." He is the patron saint of the "seeing is believing" set. He would not, could not, believe that Christ had risen from the dead unless he probed the nail-marks in his hands; unless he put his hand into the wounded side of Christ. Thomas was not deaf to the news that the other disciples were telling him about having seen the Lord, but perhaps he was blind. Like a blind person reading the resurrection story in braille, Thomas had to touch the wounds on the body of Christ.

Let's not be too harsh with his response. Maybe he was on to something. Maybe we will not see the risen Christ in one another until we see and touch each other's wounds. And since we cannot see or touch another's wounds until we have first traced the scars on our own hearts, we won't be able to breathe together from these common wounds until we touch the crucified and risen Christ in the palms of our own hands, feel the ache in our own sides, become intimate with our own wounds.

Yet when we do, we might, like Disbelieving Thomas, give voice to the most profound Christological statement in all of Scripture, "My Lord and my God." We will come to know the presence of the Risen One in the intimacy of our own wounds.

This is what we do in the conspiracy of compassion: We probe the wounds of the risen Christ. We allow the gentle Spirit of Jesus to breathe upon our wounds. We listen for the name of Jesus when we read our own wounds.

The Bond of Learning Compassion

Someone has said that we can forget those with whom we have laughed but we can never forget those with whom we have cried. Once people have suffered together, there is a bond that can never be broken, a link that time cannot weaken, a connection that distance cannot destroy.

Remember the story of Jesus being called by Martha and Mary after their brother Lazarus died. The story is so poignant and powerful because it touches at the very core of compassion. Jesus wept at the tomb of his friend because of his deep love for Lazarus and for Martha and Mary. Though he knew Lazarus would walk away from the tomb, for a brief moment he imagined what life would be like without him. Jesus wept because he saw the pain and anguish the death of Lazarus had caused in Martha and Mary and the others.

Even as he told them, "I am the resurrection and the life; the one who believes in me, though he should die, yet shall he live" (Jn. 11: 25-26), even though he reassured them with the promise of everlasting life and showed them the power of God to raise the dead to life, still "Jesus wept" (Jn. 11: 35). Perhaps the shortest and most striking verse in all of the Scriptures: "Jesus wept." He chose to mourn with those who were mourning, to suffer with those who were in pain, to weep with those who were weeping. Jesus was free enough to cry. Like Peter, in his tears the seeds of transformation and triumph sprouted from the ground of love.

It would have been much safer to leave the stone in place. It would have been less threatening to keep the stench and decay of death imprisoned in the tomb. When Jesus told them, "Take away the stone," the people were frightened. They were afraid of the smell of death.

This is our experience today: We want to keep the stone in place. We want to keep our distance from death. We turn our backs and walk away and so keep death in its place. We see this in the way we treat our old, our weak, our wounded. Our pace quickens when we see the homeless sleeping in gutters. We avoid certain places in the city because they are too dangerous, too deadly. We see it in our funeral ritual as we take the dead to a special place, have an expert put makeup on the corpse and dress the body in a new suit so we can say, "Doesn't he look good?" as we pass by the open casket.

When Jesus shouted, "Lazarus, come out!" his voice echoed through time and bounced off the walls in the halls of heaven. And when old Lazarus came shuffling out of that tomb, looking like a mummy all wrapped up in linen, the people could not believe their eyes! He was dead and now he was alive! It was so astounding, so astonishing, that many came to believe in Jesus.

Of course, there were the ever-present skeptics who went off to the religious leaders to report what Jesus had done. We have inherited this skepticism. When something remarkable occurs, the first thing we do is call a meeting, get all the facts and submit them to the "authorities"! It is as if we are saying, "Resurrection, since it is beyond the realm of our reason, must be against the law!"

But whose law? Certainly not the law of God. Creation reminds us of that. It is our law that life violates. Human law. Our world is crammed with rules and regulations we teach one another from birth about who to trust and who not to trust. We are constrained as to whom to stay away from because of the color of their skin or their political ideology or their sexual orientation or the language they speak or the place in the city where they live. These are the laws that keep us apart. These are the views that build barriers. These are the rules that bind us.

"Unbind him," Jesus told them, "and let him go" (Jn. 11: 44). Jesus taps the world on the shoulder and says, "I'm cutting in. You've danced with death long enough. I am the resurrection and the life, and I want to dance with you!"

This is the bond that can never be broken. It is the blood bond between God and humanity. The more we are willing to be free of all those human constraints, like pride and prejudice, vengeance and vindictiveness, envy and aggression, that keep us in straitjackets, making it hard to breathe, the more we will learn how to dance with life. When we are willing to take the shroud of death away from our faces, we will see our world with new eyes. With eyes of faith. With eyes of compassion.

Ablaze with Enthusiasm

Our desire to suffer with others, to gift one another with tenderness, mercy and affection, means we are also willing to congratulate one another. Literally, the word "congratulations" means "with joy." To congratulate others for an accomplishment or an achievement is to share their joy. For some unknown reason, we have learned that if someone else achieves something, we are somehow diminished. Envy seeps into our bones. But seeing with new eyes and loving with new hearts inspires us to celebrate others' joy. It leads us to make their joy our own with the same conviction we wish to make their suffering our own. In doing this, we celebrate the bonds of friendship and make those bonds even stronger.

This is a quality of our conspiracy of compassion that we must not overlook. Our solidarity with those who suffer enables us to also share their joy when hope is born. When small victories are won, when triumphs eclipse tragedies, when fidelity replaces flight, there is more than enough reason to rejoice.

What a party they must have had in Bethany that day when Lazarus came out of his tomb! Though his legs must have ached from being wrapped up for so long, I bet his legs were sore even more from the dancing he did that evening on the patio! And I'm sure Jesus was no wallflower either. I can just see Martha coming to Jesus around midnight and saying, "You know, Lord, we were not expecting a party tonight and we have run out of wine."

"No problem," Jesus would say, "remember Cana!"

The Spirit of God will not allow us to be lax in celebrating the presence of compassion in our lives. With boundless energy and unbridled enthusiasm we will dance up a storm that will shake the foundations of our houses, and our souls, and cause others to say, "They must all be drunk!" Indeed we should be, just like those first disciples were. Intoxicated with the news that death has no power over us! We are people of life!

The Spirit of Jesus has sparked a revolution that knows no boundaries. He emptied himself and allowed God to fill him with the courage to embrace the cross. Jesus was not a passive spectator in God's plan of loving the world into rebirth. Rather, in his active abandonment to God's will, he showed us the way to make the reign of God a reality in our day.

We do this by resisting all that is evil, all that is against creation, all that seeks to escape the shadow of the cross. We do this because we know that the shadow of the cross is created by the light of resurrection.

We do this because we know that resurrection, not the tomb, is our destiny. We do this because we know that community, not alienation, is our commission; that compassion, not indifference, is our common call.

We do this because we believe that the most important beatitude was not included in the Sermon on the Mount but was delivered in that brief homily in an upper room when Jesus said to Thomas, "Blest are they who do not see and yet believe (Jn. 20: 29)."

Blest are we because we believe in the presence of the crucified but risen Christ living among us.

Blest are we because we are willing to read the wounds on the body of Christ we call the church today and believe that resurrection is not only possible, it's a promise.

Blest are we because we are committed to being palm readers and promise seekers: We are willing to read the wounded palms, trace the scarred hearts, touch the open sides and see the promise that we seek. This promise gives us a reason to rejoice even in the pain of such spiritual pursuits.

Blest are we because we believe in a God of second chances and second winds — a God who understands our losses and doesn't condemn our fears. After all, even those first disciples in that upper room after having seen the risen Lord, after having inhaled the breath of life, after having received the Holy Spirit, still kept the door locked. The Gospel says that when Jesus reappeared a week later to show Thomas his wounds, the door where the newborn disciples were still hiding was still locked. Blessed, indeed, are we who believe in a God who is patient with our fragile attempts at remembering community, remembering how to breathe, even as we try to forget our fears.

Blest are we because we have found new hope in old wounds, new life in empty tombs, new joy in old friends who gather around our table to tell the stories once again.

Blest are we when we take the time to listen for the sound of Jesus' name in the palm of our hands, in the depths of our hearts, in the wounds of our lives.

Yes, blest are we when we are willing to take another's sorrow and another's joy as our own, when we are willing to let another suffer and celebrate with us.

Blest are we when we are willing to bear the name of Christ and be convicted not of the crimes of complacency but the crimes of compassion.

Then we can truly say: The conspiracy is on!

Epilogue

The Breath of Peace: Conspiring for Life

On my thirty-first birthday, my brother Ed wrote me a letter. He didn't write often, so it was a special gift and I saved it. I did not realize then, of course, that by saving it I would have a part of Ed for as long as I lived. I read some of it during the homily at his funeral. His words speak with an eloquence now that echoes in his absence. He had evidently been going through some of the scrapbooks of articles Mom had saved when I wrote for the diocesan newspaper in Kansas City.

"I can see after reading your articles," Ed wrote, "that we share the same thoughts and memories of our adventure in life and some of the wonderful people we have lived with and loved for many years." He concluded with a sentiment that summed up his care: "Anytime you want to go down to the lake is fine, Joe, and I hope you can make it as often as possible...feel free to use anything that might make your stay more pleasurable. Love, Ed."

Rereading that letter shortly after I arrived back at my parish in Sedalia after hearing the news that Ed was dead, it occurred to me that in his own simple way he was telling me what he thought of me and the family. He wanted to make life more pleasurable for us. He didn't want to burden us.

Could that have been the reason he took his own life?

When we were growing up, Ed was the one we all looked up to. He was the oldest, and his zest for living was exhausting. Whatever he tried (and no challenge seemed too great), he achieved. From those days in his youth when he was a Khoury League All-Star and played in the all-star game at Busch Stadium in St. Louis, through his years as a scout when his leadership abilities began to blossom and he gained confidence in himself, through his years in the National Guard, I looked up to Ed and whispered to myself, "That man is a success." My pride in him grew. And so did my admiration for his ability to keep all the clunkers of cars I had over the years running. It was sheer magic. From fishing to water-skiing; from bowling to pinochle, Ed enjoyed life and did things well.

But more than what he did, it was who he was that made his mark on our lives. When he bought that place at the lake, his excitement and pride knew no bounds. He worked tirelessly to make the place his own — not only for himself, but for us, his family. He was always gracious and enjoyed having people use his place. We always felt at home. It was his way of reminding us that he loved us. That he cared for us. That he only wanted us to be happy, to feel at home, at peace.

What I remember about Ed — his patience especially during the years of illness, his gentle disposition, his quite nature — live on now that he is gone. We take that with us, and nothing, not even death, can separate us from those qualities we loved and admired in Ed. With God's help, we keep them alive in our lives by becoming a little more patient under trial; a little more gentle in our relationships with each other; a little more quiet and tender amid the noise and confusion that make up so much of our lives.

For the last ten years of his life, we saw the torment etched in Ed's face and often felt powerless to know how to help him. But now we trust that Ed is in God's hands — the loving hands of a compassionate creator — and no more torment will touch him. We hold onto the promise that Ed has found the peace he had been desperately seeking.

When people ask me, "When did you become a priest?" I may answer "June 5, 1982." But if I'm honest, I know that's not true. I was ordained in 1982, but I now believe that I started becoming a priest on June 8, 1987, a little more than five years after my ordination. All the philosophy and theology, the education and ministry preparation that went into my being ordained a priest had not prepared me for the feeling of helplessness I experienced when my brother Ed committed suicide.

We grow in our understanding of what it means to be priestly, compassionate people from the crosses we carry. I really didn't begin to grasp the meaning of compassion until that day I received the call from my sister that Ed was dead. Though my family had experienced other sorrows and setbacks before, Ed's illness and death deepened our identity as carriers of the cross. During that week, as we stood as a family around the cross, in our shared suffering we went beneath the surface to a new understanding of love and relationship. Our faith in God and in one another was now fashioned by our loss, and we found a measure of freedom to love in a way we had never known before. There was nothing we could do to ease this sorrow except to try to stay close to one another, catching each other's tears and breathing into each other's wounds. Of course, in the decade following Ed's death we have often returned to the surface in our relating with one another. Yet because we have been to the depth of our shared sorrow, because we have touched this wound of our deepest pain, we can breathe a little easier, and more truly, in each other's company.

Our consolation in these ten years following Ed's death has been the compassion we have received from so many. We have not carried the burden of sorrow alone. Especially in those days following Ed's death, the gentle hand of God moved among us through those people who knew Ed and who came to share our grief. They touched our hearts with their prayers and wiped our tears with their compassion.

"Ed's Place." That sign at the lake which speaks of welcome still remains. But we trust that now Ed has finally found the peace he never knew at his place at the lake. And I am convinced that at long last Ed is free. Free and at peace. The memories that mingle with our tears remind us that Ed's spirit and love for us will shine on in our minds, in our hearts and in our relationships with each other. Ed touched our lives and left an imprint of love. Through the resurrection of Jesus we can be sure of this promise: We shall meet again — not at Ed's place at the lake, but at an even better place: the dwelling place prepared for us by Jesus.

In the meantime, I choose to leave the wound caused by his death open, hoping that it will continue to teach me how to meet others in their pain. And in our common wounds, we breathe together, conspiring for life, for love, for compassion.